Praise for
CELEBRATE SELLING THE CONSULTATIVE-RELATIONSHIP WAY

"What's better than getting sales tips from a top, nationally recognized sales trainer? Getting sales tips from eleven top, nationally recognized sales trainers. A wonderful concept with tremendous results."
> —Robert L. Jolles, *Customer Centered Selling*

"Celebrate Selling the Consultative-Relationship Way is a book for anybody who sells. Lots of 'ah ha's' and insights . . . . It's a great course and a great refresher. Read it and get better."
> — Larry Wilson, founder and vice chairman
> Pecos River® Division, Aon Consulting
> *Stop Selling, Start Partnering*

"This is a book about winning customers, not orders. Highly readable, with illustrative anecdotes, it guides the reader in how to build relationships with customers, to be a consultant and even more to your customers! A must for small and large businesses."
> —Herman Holtz, *How to Succeed as an Independent Consultant*

"The new world of business demands salespeople who listen, understand, and deliver. This book is a road map to success."
> — Barbara Geraghty, *Visionary Selling*

"Consultative-relationship selling isn't just for those selling consulting services; everyone who sells a product, service, organization, or idea can profit from these methods. By establishing consultative relationships with your prospects, using the techniques outlined in this book, you can overcome buyers' inherent distrust of salespeople and instead gain their confidence, respect, friendship, and—most importantly—their business."
> — Bob Bly, *Selling Your Services*

"These days, it's not enough to just 'win.' This book shows you how to 'win-win' by celebrating selling!"
> —Louis Patler, *If It Ain't Broke . . . Break It!*

"Guaranteed to make your sales soar. Your relationships with your customers will be a real jubilee."
> — Salli Rasberry, *Advertising without Marketing*

"Consultative-relationship selling is a virtual smorgasbord of delightful and successful ways to approach sales in a practical, 21st-century way. I recommend it highly and enthusiastically."
> — Bill Brooks, *Niche Selling*

". . . a great read for anyone involved in business-to-business sales. If readers take the advice found in this book, they should reap immediate rewards for their businesses and themselves."
> — Jon Lowder, *Relationship Marketing Report*

"I have read every book ever published on sales. Rick has done an exceptional job of pulling together the "best of the best" when it comes to relationship selling. Must reading for the salesperson of the 21st century."
 —Tim Connor, CSP, *Soft Sell*

"This book covers what I've found really works in almost 40 years of serious selling. Selling shouldn't be about techniques, especially closing techniques, but rather about customers' needs. This book helps you think beyond the norm—beyond your horizons to use creativity and ideas to build friendships—and business."
 —Jack Sweeney, CRMC, sales consultant

"New approaches to selling for the new millennium! . . . . contains timely, sensible information from the best sales minds out there."
 — Jerry Ann Jinnett, *Target Marketing*

"The day of 'hit and run,' 'love 'em and leave 'em' selling are history. This book is a treasury of strategies for finding customer needs and building relationships."
 — Jerry R. Wilson, CSP, *Word-of-Mouth Marketing*

" . . . a really valuable collection of tips and techniques."
 — Lawrence M. Kohn, *Selling with Honor:*
 Strategies for Selling without Selling Your Soul

"Finally! A book that provides a step by step guide to win-win selling. In this case, the readers emerge as the biggest winners. They walk away with valuable 'how-to's' and insights on opening valuable long-term relations with their clients."
 — Fred Berns, *Sell Yourself! 501 Ways to Get*
 Them to Buy from You

"This book is packed with information on how to establish relationships with prospects and customers and on how to help them improve profits with consultative selling. If you're in sales, read it and learn how you can profit by helping your customers succeed."
 — Michael Michalko, *Thinkertoys (A Handbook of Business*
 Creativity) and *Cracking Creativity (The Secrets of*
 Creative Geniuses)

"Provides a new selling paradigm and a set of practical tools that will give you the competitive edge."
 — David Brandt, *Sacred Cows Make the Best Burgers*

" . . . . provides a new look at the topic of selling. In Rick Crandall's seminars, the concept of relationship selling versus the traditional sales model has been a real eye opener for our clients and helped many small business owners change their mindsets as to how they view sales."
 — Charles Eason, director
 Napa Valley College Small Business Development Center

Celebrate Selling
the
Consultative-Relationship
Way

Featuring chapters by:

Aldonna R. Ambler • Greg Bauer • Bill Blades
Jeff Cramer • Rick Crandall • Joachim de Posada
Jerry L. Fritz • Theodore W. Garrison III • John W. Hobart
Linda M. Keats • Renee P. Walkup

Edited by Rick Crandall

Sponsored by
The Institute for Effective Sales and Marketing

Select Press
Corte Madera, CA

Select Press
P.O. Box 37
Corte Madera, CA 94976-0037
(415) 435-4461

Celebrate Selling the Consultative-Relationship Way /
Rick Crandall (editor)

ISBN 1-890777-04-8

Printed in the United States of America
10 9 8 7 6 5 4 3 2 1

Contents

PREFACE

Lots of lip service is given to building relationships with customers, consultative selling™, partnering with customers, and similar terms. Unfortunately, it is lip service, not the reality of most sales today.

The professional knows that repeat business and referrals are where 90% of successful companies' profits come from. If you're proud of what you sell, you enjoy sharing it. If that's not the way you feel about selling your products or services, get better training or get out of your business!

And How Do You Pronounce "Consultative" Anyway?

"Consultative Selling" is a trademarked term owned by Mack Hanan. He first published a book by that name in 1970.

But the important thing is how the heck do you pronounce "consultative." Mack Hanan doesn't have a strong preference. But he pronounces it as "consult" plus "ta tive" (kōn-'sîl-te-tiv). Inquiring minds wanted to know!

Chapter 1

CONSULTATIVE-RELATIONSHIP SELLING

Bill Blades

Bill Blades, CMC, CPS, is a consultant, speaker, and author. At the age of 22, he served as plant manager for a major manufacturing firm while a full-time college student. Later, while serving as vice president of sales and marketing for a food manufacturing concern, he increased sales nearly 150 percent from $13 million to $33 million in only four years. His firm was named Small Business of the Year and was always the top marketing firm in the food manufacturing area.

Mr. Blades is the author of the bestseller, *Selling: The Mother of all Enterprise*. In addition, he is featured with noted attorney F. Lee Bailey in the book *Leadership Strategists*.

One of only 51 Certified Management Consultants in the U.S. who speaks and consults with clients in the areas of sales and marketing, Mr. Blades does so with a straightforward mission statement: Our mission is to always deliver more than we promise and to serve as our clients' partners in the quest for excellence. His clients include Buick, ConAgra, GTE, and Motorola.

Bill Blades, William Blades & Associates, Ltd., 11126 East Breathless Drive, Gold Canyon, AZ 85219; phone (602) 671-3000; fax (602) 671-0926; e-mail WBlades@aol.com; www.WilliamBlades.com.

CONSULTATIVE-RELATIONSHIP SELLING

Bill Blades

"Consultative Selling replaces the traditional adversarial buyer-seller relationship with a win-win partnership in profit improvement."
—Mack Hanan, *Consultative Selling*

There is a well established methodology for selling professionally that we can all be proud to celebrate. It helps clients achieve profits—which they then share with you.

Yet, selling has had a negative image for many years because of the selfish, pushy amateurs who do anything to close sales but don't invest in building long-term relationships. The following joke captures the essence of this old make-the-sale-at-any-cost philosophy.

A salesman was killed in an accident. He meets Saint Peter who tells him that they've instituted a new program: He can choose whether he wants to go to Heaven or Hell. He says he can't make a choice because he has no first-hand information, so Saint Peter lets him visit each place. The salesman spends the first day in Heaven where everyone wears white robes and listens to lovely music, plays harps, and walks around beautiful fields. He spends the next day in Hell where there's a great party going on. The women are gorgeous, with few clothes and fewer inhibitions, the wine flows, and people are dancing and enjoying themselves. The salesman tells Saint Peter that Heaven looks nice, but Hell seems to be more his style, so that's where St. Peter sends him. When he arrives,

"This offer is void where prohibited by law."

he is immediately grabbed by demons, thrown into chains, and dangled over a hot fire! He says "It wasn't like this when I visited. What happened to the party?" The closest demon says, "Yesterday you were a prospect, today you're a customer!"

This is the image I originally had of sales. My background was in operations. When I was recruited into sales, I hesitated because I thought sales was a bad-image career.

GOOD RELATIONSHIPS = BETTER SALES

I did make the shift to sales. Because I knew nothing about the industry I was selling in, I had to work on relationship building and listen to customers. I learned from customers and became an industry "expert."

Building solid relationships with customers benefits you in three major ways. Your profits can grow as much as 100% from a 10% increase in customer retention. Your costs of marketing go down tremendously when 90% of your business is repeat and referrals. And, your customers can become "raving fans." They can generate referrals and even sell for you.

Relationship Marketing, Consultative Selling™, and Other "New Selling" Techniques

Many terms relate to the "new selling" that we advocate here. Perhaps the most general is "relationship marketing." Several books have been written using this title. They reinforce the general idea that building relationships with prospects and customers will help you be successful. But you need to go further.

An article in the *Harvard Business Review* recently complained that relationship marketing collects more information from consumers, but benefits them little. Similarly, just about all the recent sales books talk about relationship building. Yet the old manipulative sales attitude slips through in language like: "develop strategies and tactics to get others to say 'yes,'" "convince others that your product is exactly what they need," "outsmart prospects' objections," and "After you ask a closing question, Shut Up! The next person who speaks loses."

These strategies don't sound like advice for consultants, partners, and advisors with customers' interests first in their minds! I use the term "servant sales" to emphasize your obligation in the customer relationship. With servant selling, you sell and advance your own interests only by helping others achieve their goals.

The most developed term is "consultative selling"™. Mack Hanan uses it to describe a

---

One-to-One Marketing

The newest approach to building customer relationships is one-to-one marketing. The ultimate target market is one customer. And salespeople are the best people to use customer information to serve each customer personally.

"Instead of selling one product at a time to as many customers as possible . . . the one-to-one marketer uses customer databases and interactive communications to sell one customer at a time as many [customized] products and services as possible . . . over the lifetime of the customer's patronage."

—Don Peppers and Martha Rogers, *Enterprise One to One*

process in which you improve your customers' returns on investment by bringing them solutions to their problems, and then partner with them to implement the solutions. Many others continue to use this term in a more general sense of building relationships with customers and acting like a consultant.

FIVE STEPS FOR CONSULTATIVE-RELATIONSHIP SELLING

I've broken "new selling" down into five key areas, some of which are covered in detail in other chapters. These steps are:

(1) building relationships
(2) analyzing needs
(3) knowing your customers' industries
(4) generating creative ideas
(5) helping your customers succeed

If you're in sales, you should become proficient in all five areas.

Moments of Truth

Every customer contact is an opportunity to build the customer relationship. Yet most organizations waste their chances. Jan Carlzon of SAS airlines coined the term "moments of truth" to remind his employees that each and every contact with customers or prospects is an opportunity to impress them.

From each contact, customers and prospects form an impression that they will generalize to other areas of your organization. For instance, if a salesperson doesn't return calls promptly (while trying to get the order), prospects are likely to assume that if they become customers, their calls to customer service will also be neglected.

Step 1: Building Relationships

Everyone can contribute to building relationships with prospects and customers. In fact, customers are often more impressed when the person answering the phone remembers them than when a salesperson makes a bigger effort to be friendly. Everyone wants to be treated as special.

With big customers, many times the most difficult part of the relationship-building process is to convince them it's worth their while to even consider you. For every customer meeting, you should have a plan! Know what you're going to share with them, and what you're going to learn from them. If you don't know this, then you're not ready for a meeting. I used to send important prospects a three-page letter (plan) telling them, "Here's what I'm going to do to win your business, and after you hire me, here's what I'm going to do to keep it." No one had ever done this. It blew them away and resulted in lots of new customers for me.

Relationships should include as many people in the customer's company as possible. For instance, I was all ready to do business with a guy who called on me. I mentioned to my assistant how great it would be to do business with him. She said, "If you like that type!" He'd been cold to her in the waiting room, and needless to say, I didn't do business with him.

I try to spend 100% of my time with customers and prospects looking for needs to fill—especially those needs that have nothing to do with business. This builds a more real relationship. For instance, our Arizona Diamondback baseball team gear is popular all over the country. One customer told me her warehouse manager had been looking all over for a Diamondback's hat. Giving one to the customer made her warehouse manager happy, and the customer a hero. When a customer indicates an interest, I put them on the team's magazine list. Every month when it arrives, they're reminded of me. Keep your ears open for things to do for family, friends, and coworkers of your customers.

Individual differences. People are like thumbprints—no two are alike. To build relationships, you have to treat people differently! Yet

---

Include Families in Relationship Building

Thrill customers and prospects by keeping their family situations in mind. If you can make them a hero with their children by giving them a special baseball card or promotional item that they wouldn't normally have access to, then you've added to the relationship.

—*Executive Edge* newsletter

many salespeople make every sales call the same.

One method for classifying general types of behavior is the DiSC®. I am the classic High D (Dominance behavior) and High I (Influencing behavior) guy. On the S and C dimensions (Steadiness and Conscientious behaviors), I'm very low.

High D/High I people love to talk. A salesperson cannot come in and call on me, yapping away. Salespeople better be doing two things: They better give me an idea that can potentially help me—and they better get straight to the point.

An understanding of the four DiSC behavior styles—or other behavior classification systems—will allow you to tailor your approach to the individual. For instance, with the Steady-type person, you'll probably want to sit over a cup of coffee and just shoot the breeze for about five minutes before you start. With people like me, you start the first minute you get there. When you're doing new selling, you've got to be aware and use different styles for different people, even though your goal is always to build a relationship. (See Chapter 3 for more on building relationships.)

> When you're talking, you know what you know. When you're listening, you know what you know *plus* what the other person knows.
> —Old sales saying

Step 2: Analyzing Needs

Most salespeople have their talk-listen ratio out of whack. Great needs-analysis selling is:

(1) 90% asking targeted questions,

(2) listening intently to every single word, and

(3) taking great notes.

Needs-analysis selling is only 10 percent talking (on your part). People, when listening, have only a three-sentence attention span on average. If your customer or prospect has an active mind, after three or four sentences, you'd better be asking a question. Unfortunately, when a lot of a salespeople are supposedly listening to a client they're thinking, "I'll be glad when the client shuts up, so I can say something important." But a salesperson who really listens shows respect to the talker (which adds to the relationship), and also can learn more about the client's needs and motivations.

Here's an example of a "good" conversation from the client's point of view. The client says to me, "Bill, we are taking our group to Hawaii."

I've only a one-word question: "Hawaii?"

"Yeah, we're going over to Maui. It's an incentive trip."

"Incentive?"

"Yeah, every year we take the top ten . . ." and it goes on and on and on.

Often, I only respond with a one-word question. The client is happy (most people like to talk), and the one-word responses encourage the client to elaborate, which gives you more information about the client and the client's company. (See Chapter 4 for more on needs analysis.)

Needs analysis. When I do needs analysis, I will sometimes ask questions that have nothing to do with my business. A salesperson who might be selling computers might ask, "Mr. Jones, let me ask this question so that I can learn how to help you better. Could I get a copy of your mission statement?" Or the question might be, "In your business plan, or sales and marketing plan, what's the number one thing that you are going to be working on this year?" These are good business-consulting questions.

Use standard forms. I use two needs analysis forms in my business. One is for speaking and the other one is for long-term consulting projects.

Don't Sell Me . . .

People hate to buy things. They want their needs and desires satisfied. Complete the following statement: "Don't sell me [your task in concrete terms] . . . sell me [your task in abstraction]. Complete the statement ten or more times (e.g., "Don't sell me soft drinks . . . sell me fun; don't sell me soft drinks . . . sell me youth."). This exercise takes you to the essence of your product or service from a variety of emotional directions.

—Doug Hall, *Jump Start Your Brain: A Proven Method for Increasing Creativity Up to 500%*

In my absence from the office, everyone is equipped and well trained to ask the questions.

When it comes time for a long-term consulting project, I get paid to go in for three days just to ask questions. And it takes us a minimum of two days to go all the way through them. Two or three years ago, a company president in Oklahoma brought me in for a couple of days just off of my reputation. We were in the boardroom with his VPs and he said, "You haven't convinced me yet."

I said, "Sir, I've not even tried. I'm just here to find out what needs fixing. You called me in. I'm not trying to sell anything because in the medical field, prescription without diagnosis would be malpractice. Every consulting project that I do is different. It's not a canned program coming off the shelf. I need to finish asking all these questions. Then we will go back and prioritize every single thing that needs improving. Then I will know what you want me to do first."

He said, "I like it. Will you teach our salespeople how to do this?"

I said, "Sir, I will. I can't tell you when. It depends on your priority list."

Step 3: Knowing Your Customer's Industry

This is one of the areas in which this book can't help you. You have to do your own homework in each industry and company you serve. Broad knowledge from many areas can be useful but when most people have a problem, they want an expert in that area. They don't want to have to bring you up to speed on their

Build Your Expertise

For each industry that is important to you, do extra homework on your own time to understand issues and enhance your credibility.

- Read the trade magazines that your customers read.
- Build files on key topics in each industry.
- Go to industry trade shows.
- Do surveys of customers' concerns.

time! That's why focused, niche marketing is so powerful.

Educate yourself about both what your company sells and about your customers' industries. People who are serious about their businesses know more than their competitors. They usually read more than anybody else. They don't read between the hours of 8 a.m. and 5 p.m, but they read at night and on weekends.

Work harder for yourself than you do for your boss. Read, read, read so that you can find things that will be of interest to a client. Mark Twain said, "The man who does not read has no advantage over the man who cannot." In other words, the books and the magazines you don't read may hurt you.

Step 4: Be Creative

The three-page letter that I sent to important prospects got their attention because it was creative in addition to promising a plan of action.

Jeff Tanner, of the Center for Professional Selling at Baylor University, tells about Cliff, a salesman with a promotional products company. Creativity is important in this field because you have to help your clients get attention from *their* prospects. And most competitors imprint the same items, so there are few

---

Attention-Getting Gifts

For some business people, a single account can be worth millions of dollars. When this is the case, there will be lots of other salespeople trying to reach the decision makers.

The West Coast trust division of a bank had been trying to bid on managing an investment portfolio for a doctors' group for years, but they couldn't get an appointment to make a presentation. They knew which doctors made the investment decisions for the group. So, they spent about $100 apiece on old-fashioned stopwatches and had them gift-wrapped for each doctor. Then they hired a private detective to find their home addresses.

Each gift was sent to the home, where it wouldn't be screened by an office manager. With it was a note, "Please time me with a stopwatch. I'd like to make a presentation. It will take less than five minutes and I won't take longer unless invited to say more." This dramatic gimmick paid off and the rep got the appointment.

—Rick Crandall, *1001 Ways to Market Your Services: Even If You Hate to Sell*

differences between the products from different companies.

Cliff had a dozen important prospects who wouldn't see him. He had pizza cutters imprinted with each prospect's name on one side of the handle and his name and company name on the other side. He had Domino's Pizza deliver each cutter, along with a pizza, just before lunch. Each box had a letter attached asking for a chance at "a slice" of the prospect's business. His creativity paid off. Ten of 12 prospects called for an appointment!

Step 5: Helping Your Customers Succeed

The first four steps of "new selling" are all designed to help you provide value to your customers. By building relationships, you win their trust to take the relationship further. You analyze their needs and apply your knowledge of their industry and your creativity to come up with solutions for them. Then your solutions help them succeed, which builds the long-term business which is profitable for you.

Boost your customers' profits. What can you give your clients that will help them? Here's a creative idea. I often speak to my clients' customers. I will do a "CEO conference." My clients invite CEOs both from firms that buy a lot from them and from firms that are buying nothing. We strategically seat the CEOs around the breakfast tables so each table has a mixture of CEOs who can give testimonials about different aspects of the client's

A Mission to Help

Harry Bullis, former chairman of the board of General Mills, would tell his salespeople, "Forget about the sales you hope to make and concentrate on the service you want to render . . . . I tell our salespeople that if they would start out each morning with the thought, 'I want to help as many people as possible today,' instead of 'I want to make as many sales as possible today,' they would find a more easy and open approach to their buyers and they would make more sales. The person who goes out to help people to a happier and easier way of life is exercising the highest type of salesmanship."

services. I tell the client: "Do not pass out literature. Say nothing about your company. I will brag about you one time when I'm talking about value added."

After I finish my talk, the client visits each table and says, "Folks, we want to thank you for coming. We hope this was everything that we said it would be and I hope you'll stay and chat. Thank you very much." It's totally soft sell. The guests are thinking, "Wait a minute. Where's the hook?" People see that we're investing time and money to bring value to them and start viewing us as their partner.

SUMMARY

Today in sales training, lots of people give lip service to customer-focused, service-oriented selling. But when you look at the content of most of the material, it goes through the old steps of presenting, overcoming objections, and closing sales.

If you want to be a professional salesperson, you need to be proud of what you sell and comfortable about your ability to help the people you work with. The tools in this book will help keep you on the track of "new selling." It's up to you to do the hard work to stay there.

In my sales training, I tell people that sales training by itself does not work, salespeople do.

You've got to do a lot of follow-up. You've got to hold people accountable for X number of new skills. You've got to monitor like crazy. That way, the investment comes back; otherwise, most people will keep acting just as they did last week.

When we educate salespeople individually, we give them new assignments based on their own personality profiles by profession. We might require them to learn 12 new skills a quarter. Then they're professionals who are investing in themselves and they're better able to help clients.

Work hard on developing yourself. Go the extra mile for clients by delivering unheard-of value. And never stop. It's called professional sales.

BURST INTO ACTION

"If you really want to do something, you'll find a way; if you don't, you'll find an excuse."
—*Forbes* magazine

(1) Change your emphasis from *closing* sales to *opening* long-term business relationships.

(2) Start gathering information about your customers' and prospects' business and personal interests.

(3) Study the personal styles of the people you come in regular contact with and see if it helps you relate to them.

(4) Do research with your best customers to see how they analyze their needs.

(5) Go to your clients' trade shows, or *their* clients' shows.

(6) Go to the library and find magazines that would give you ideas for your clients. Then subscribe to some. (Many trade magazines are free.)

(7) Develop something to creatively set you apart.

(8) Ask good customers about how you could help them with their customers.

MANAGE CUSTOMER RELATIONSHIPS AT HIGHER LEVELS

Jeff Cramer

Jeff Cramer
is president of the Sonoran
Retreat for Executive Performance, an international pro-
vider of leadership development and training for management, sales, and
customer-service professionals. Organizations like GTE, Digital Equipment, and
IBM use programs from the Sonoran Retreat. Also a founding director of the Sales
Professionals of America, he has published a variety of articles on sales
management practices and sales-force development.

Prior to cofounding the Sonoran Retreat, Mr. Cramer served as vice
president of marketing for CyCare Systems, a top NYSE computer software and
services provider to the healthcare industry. His more than 20 years of experience
includes sales, management, and executive-level positions with leading corporations such as IBM, Digital Equipment, and Oracle. His educational background
includes postgraduate studies at Harvard University.

As an active member of the American Management Association and the
National Speakers Association, Mr. Cramer's commitment to excellence continues to make a recognized difference in the industry. The fulfillment he has
experienced as an expert in his field is only rivaled by his enjoyment of family
and friends.

Jeff Cramer, Sonoran Retreat for Executive Performance, 7950 E. Redfield Rd.,
Suite 170, Scottsdale, AZ 85260; phone 602-348-9799; fax 602-348-9899;
e-mail jeff@sonoranretreat.com.

MANAGE CUSTOMER RELATIONSHIPS AT HIGHER LEVELS

Jeff Cramer

"Professional sales is moving fast from the vendor level to consultants and trusted advisors treating each customer as a target market of one."

—Don Peppers

All of us in this book agree that building relationships with prospects and customers is the key to success. In thinking about your relationship goals, it is important to know that there are levels beyond consultant that you can achieve.

Not just any relationship will do if you want to be a super achiever. Since your success is directly proportionate to the quality of the relationship you maintain with each of your customers, you'll need to constantly monitor and improve your connections to customers.

There are at least six levels of possible relationships between salespeople and customers. Going from lowest to highest level, they are:

(1) vendor

(2) solutions provider

(3) consultant

(4) team member

(5) partner

(6) advisor

As you move up to Team-Member status or above, your customers become advocates for you. These raving fans produce many profitable referrals.

CHANGING YOUR MODEL

I'm about to ask you one of the most important questions you've ever considered with regard to your business relationships: Do customers think of you as being almost indispensable? If you answered no, why not? That's the position where you can be of most benefit to your customers.

Learning how to manage your outcomes by elevating your relationships is like experiencing a continual climb to success, with rewards that just keep on coming! If you discover a huge discrepancy between the way customers perceive you now and how you would like to be perceived, it's time to climb Led Zeppelin's *Stairway to Heaven*— by building your relationships.

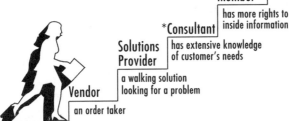

Advisor
is empowered to make decisions and give advice

Partner
is extremely trustworthy; actively listens

Team Member
has more rights to inside information

*Consultant
has extensive knowledge of customer's needs

Solutions Provider
a walking solution looking for a problem

Vendor
an order taker

*Ideally, you should enter all your business relationships no lower than the Consultant level.

Before you can begin climbing that success stairway, you'll need to understand the levels and identify the success you experience with each customer. So, let's break it down a little further and examine perceptions, outcomes, resistance, identifying behaviors, and differentiating characteristics of each level—beginning with the lowest level: Vendor.

Vendor

To start your relationships at this level is a mistake. Stuck at this level, the salesperson is perceived as an order taker, a carrier of commodities. There is no customer loyalty because none has been earned. The salesperson's limited knowledge of the customer and the customer's company offers no leverage during what usually turns into a difficult negotiating process. Since competition is high and accessibility to the customer is low, cost concessions are commonly the end result, creating lower profit margins and fewer referrals for the salesperson.

It's fairly easy to identify this relationship level—you're feeling the economic and emotional crunch at the bottom of the pile. You ask few questions, offer limited information, present products and services instead of customer benefits, and make little attempt to understand the customer by demonstrating active listening. You may also develop defensive speech and mannerisms due to lack of trust on the part of your customer.

What differentiates Vendors from the competition? Nothing! They may be creating a memorable moment, but is that the moment of magic they intended to make? Probably not! About the

---

Salespeople Are Not Building Relationships

Salespeople greatly overestimate the quality of the relationships they have with customers. That is the conclusion drawn from a study in which 173 business people purchased from 193 sales reps and both groups rated the quality of the salesperson-customer relationship.

—Hawes et al., *Psychological Reports,* Vol. 72, pp. 607-614.

only thing that differentiates Vendors is price and a negative mindset or intent to put their own needs before those of the customers.

Solutions Provider

At this level, the customer views the salesperson as a solution looking for a problem. While salespeople at this level have more knowledge and skills, and are able to address common and generic needs, resistance remains high. Salespeople are usually involved in a more complex sale that keeps them struggling through the negotiation process. There is more to differentiate them from their competitors. Accessibility to the customer is a bit higher than at the Vendor level, but there is still much room for improvement. The salesperson still feels the need to make cost concessions, which can substantially lower profit margins.

If you're a Vendor on the move, you'll recognize yourself at this level when you find yourself asking more questions of your customers. The problem comes when you don't know how to implement strategic responses that maximize customer benefits. Because the Solutions Provider is still only a marginal listener, he or she is not capable of identifying specific benefits and building confidence in the customer's mind. The Solutions Provider offers more information, but the relationship has been built on a fragile foundation.

What differentiates Solutions Providers is usually not great selling skills or

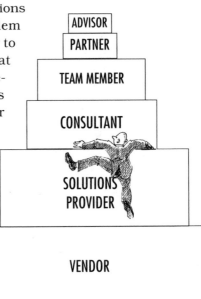

ADVISOR

PARTNER

TEAM MEMBER

CONSULTANT

SOLUTIONS PROVIDER

VENDOR

an ability to sell with empathy and caring. They haven't given enough attention to the needs and wants of their customers to see things from that perspective. Most of the time, Solutions Providers may be more desirable than their competitors simply because of better or more diverse lines of products. When the same products can be carried by many different companies, the salesperson will want to have something that makes them more distinguishable.

> A purchase decision is not a decision to have an "affair," but a decision to have a "marriage." This requires of the would-be seller a new orientation and a new strategy.
> —Tom Peters

Consultant

Consultant is the minimum relationship level for creating effective and long-lasting business. Because salespeople on this level have much greater knowledge and are focused on what's best for the customer, the resistance to desired outcomes is much lower. Less negotiation, less competition, more accessibility to the customer, and more trust in the relationship generate greater profit margins and higher year-end yields.

Solutions Providers who are moving up will be able to identify that they are at this level when they are still asking questions, but have learned to target customer needs and wants, and thus respond with much more insight. Consultants link products and services to specific customer benefits. You demonstrate more confidence and self-assuredness in your abilities to make perfect matches between products and customers when you become an evaluative listener.

What does reaching the Consultant level mean? A transformation for you and your businesses, a change of intent and mindset to customer-focused sales. What differentiates you from other hungry salespeople in your industry? Service mindset and selfless intent!

Team Member

At this level, you are a member of the team, not just an outsider. The customer views you as a team player. You are perceived as having an increased awareness of internal company politics and a shared expertise with others on the team. Because of this, you are given greater opportunities to gain inside information. Like the inside team members, you are considered trustworthy and loyal to the customer and his or her company.

So, what could a salesperson at this level do to better manage outcomes? Not a lot; you're definitely on your way up. Shaky negotiations are replaced by mutually respectful and honest discussions. Competition is almost nil; you're one of them, now! Because you are perceived as important to the customer, you hold a position of power and are less likely to feel as though you have to make concessions in order to maintain the relationship. It doesn't take long before team members share your expertise with another team within the organization. Then it's "Hello referrals!"

You'll know you're a Team Member because your insightful questions demonstrate a thorough knowledge of many different departments and their areas of dissatisfaction. Team Members have that "we" mentality when presenting product benefits, responding strategically and keeping their eyes on the bigger picture. Then they are able to satisfy many needs of various

> ### From the Inside-Out
>
> Salespeople can operate immediately as team members if they are ex-employees of the company to whom they are now selling. They have already achieved trust and are perceived as working as much for the "ex-company" as the company they now sell for.

"We're all team players here, Furgis. Miss Parmenter will break you in."

departments at maximum efficiency because of that "big picture" capability.

What differentiates the Team Member from his or her competition? Active listening and trust! You are flexible and adaptable to different behavioral styles, so you blend perfectly with the group. When the team message has been shared, not only are you able to appreciate the speaker, but you can also build value in the message.

Partner

Although many salespeople like to apply the Partner label to themselves, salespeople at this level are, unfortunately, few and far between. Partners are extremely trustworthy because they have proven themselves to have unselfish motives. Customers don't question partners, but instead show them more of the customers' personal, positional, and business needs and wants. As long as the Partner maintains this level of relationship, competition doesn't exist in the minds of their customers. And—forget about negotiations—they are replaced by conversation with a trusted friend.

Salespeople on this level go far beyond what is asked for, or even identified, by the customer. They encourage and inspire; they actively listen. They are confident enough to remain a professional, generally admitting when they are being asked to accomplish a task that is outside their realm of expertise. Your business is based on an open, honest, and fearless relationship. The success of your customer is taken personally. In many cases the Partner becomes a close friend, invited to social gatherings and special events in the personal lives of their customers.

What differentiates you from the competition is that you are privy to information made available only to those at that highest level, which excludes most of the competition. Because of the trust level, the Partners' customers don't judge them nega-

> We are in the midst of a revolution . . . those organizations and individuals who can create new relationships with customers will find themselves with unimagined competitive advantage. Those who don't will lose.
> —Larry Wilson, *Stop Selling, Start Partnering*

tively for what they can't do, but rather positively for knowing exactly whom to recommend for those services they can't provide.

Advisor

Salespeople on this highest of levels are mutually empowered to make decisions and give advice. They are comfortable with being maverick thinkers and are, in fact, rewarded for speaking candidly and with absolute authority. There is nothing at this level of the relationship to keep the Advisor from a successful outcome. Instead, they are able to move independently, finding the directions that best suit their customers. The customers often outsource projects that are completely under the control of the Advisor. Without consulting upper management, the Advisor has the authority to act, do, and follow through, bringing to executive management the bottom-line results. There is no need to negotiate here; the customer will almost always take the Advisor's recommendations with few questions.

How will you know you are perceived as an Advisor? Since the focus is always on the relationship, the Advisor is allowed to speak frankly without fear of rejection. Customer questions are not about your capabilities, but more to understand your feelings and seek out your opinions. "What would you consider the best approach?" Or, "How do you feel about changing our supplier?" Congratulations! As an Advisor, you have become one of the Untouchables. Remember that movie

The Marginal Man

Relationship-oriented salespeople fit the old sociological concept of "marginal man." You are not an actual member of your customer's company so they can treat you like an outsider. Yet you are seen as a representative of your customers within your own company, so you are not a full member there either. In fact, you are often seen as an irritant within your company when you protect your customers' interests and become their advocate.

Technical Salespeople

Engineers and other technical people with no sales backgrounds can often achieve great things in sales. One reason is because they automatically approach the sales situation as consultants, partners, or advisors. When working with other technical people, they think of themselves as one of "them." They act that way, and are often accepted that way by the customers.

where the good guys walk tall and come out the winners? That's you—the Advisor.

What makes the difference in establishing yourself at the highest relationship level is not luck or even experience; it's mostly due to your high energy and endless effort. Investing that extraordinary effort requires 100% responsibility on your part. Don't expect your customers to meet you halfway. Why should they work to send you the business? Give 100% of yourself, expect 100% of the business, and soon you'll be climbing that stairway. You've got to *know* . . .

- the customer
- the customer's company and industry
- your company
- your products and services
- your competition
- yourself

Remember, you'll get fewer "no's" when you're in the *know*!

STARTING YOUR CLIENTS UP THE RELATIONSHIP STAIRWAY

Constant movement up that stairway is key to establishing yourself as an Advisor to your customers. Stuck in a rut? Then stop focusing on what you are doing wrong and, instead, look at a business relationship where you are perceived as an Advisor. Then take a closer look at what you are doing right. Next, do that same right thing over and over again.

In order to climb that stairway to successful business relationships, you have to consider your strengths in the following four areas:

- competence
- trust
- likability
- value

Competence

How much do you know about your customer's business? Can you actually listen to the challenges that a CEO is facing and understand them? And, when you hear some of those challenges, do you know their effect on bottom-line profits? If you know the inner workings of your own company and your customers' companies, you'll be able to marshal the resources that will allow customers to capture their fair share, and in some cases, the lion's share, of the marketplace. In the process, you're viewed as the hero!

Trust

When you have been recommended by another customer who perceives you as an Advisor, your plan of action automatically comes with a higher value and usually can support a higher profit margin. After all, you have proven yourself with others in the industry and perhaps other departments within the same company. Trust comes by doing more than just meeting customer expectations—you've got to be constantly on the lookout for ways to exceed them. The way you do that is to focus on strategically listening to your customer's plan

Multiple Roles for Relationship-Style Salespeople

- administrator
- coach
- consultant
- facilitator
- influencer
- motivator
- needs analyst
- networker
- objective observer
- partner
- problem solver
- researcher
- sounding board
- strategist
- technical expert

and implementing one of your own that offers even more than the customer dreamed possible.

Likability

Plain and simple—do your customers like you? Why? Are you flexible and adaptable to the behavior and needs of your customers? Are you able to do business just as successfully with people whose behavior is not that which you prefer for yourself? Studies suggest that personalities can be divided into at least four categories. If you only work with customers who are similar in personality style to yours, 75% of the population will miss the benefits you could provide. There's value in being versatile!

Value

Value is what ties together all of your strengths in the eyes of your customers and creates a need for them to do business with you and your company. Customers will be asking "How much? How soon? How sure?" That's what they want to know: "How much will I be able to gain by doing business with you and your company? How soon will it happen? How sure are you that it will happen?"

One of the best ways to address this on the higher levels of business relationships is to show your prospects and customers companies within their industry that have greatly benefited by doing business with you. Bring in third-party testimoni- · als. (Sounds great in theory, but you probably won't have any to show—if you do, you're on your way up!) Testimonials come from long-standing, mutually beneficial relationships, and they are not a part of the lower-level equation.

Create Raving Fans

Customers become raving fans only when they know they can count on you time and time again.

Exceeding expectations is important, but it's even more important to consistently meet expectations. Meet first. Exceed second.

—Ken Blanchard and Sheldon Bowles, *Raving Fans*

SUMMARY

Working up into higher relationship levels requires patience, effort, and a little bit of luck. But, you make your own luck when you are alert to opportunities to demonstrate your sincerity in your relationships.

Many of you may be thinking that experience has a great deal to do with your ability to attain higher levels—not so! What elevates you the quickest is intent and effort. If you are determining solutions based on the customer's agenda instead of your own, and if you are demonstrating a high level of knowledge and desire, then you are well on your way to Advisor selling!

One way to climb quickly is through 3×3 selling (contacting at least three different people within the organization in three different departments). It's much like 4×4 driving. Because you can create selling opportunities, you can go places that were inaccessible to you before, and you have less resistance in the form of negotiations. You have less resistance and fewer chances of getting stuck at one level. Let's face it, the higher the relationship level, the more time the customer and his or her company has invested in you. When that happens, customers are less likely to drop that relationship and start all over again with another salesperson.

Let me leave you with one last thought. When you maintain higher levels of business relationships, selling is just a *whole lot more fun*! With the higher levels come more responsibilities, like a need for ongoing education and training. Top-producing salespeople realize that knowledge is not an event—it's a state of mind; the more you know, the

---

One-to-One Selling

Customers invest time in the relationship to "train" you to their system and needs. Customize for each customer so that switching to another supplier would cost them great inconvenience in bringing the new company up the learning curve.

—Don Peppers and Martha Rogers,
The One to One Future: Building Relationships One Customer at a Time

more you know you need to know!

Want to change your relationships? Great! Change your mindset; open your mind to a higher state of learning. Constantly seek people and situations that will bring you growth, a broader understanding of business, and a thirst for more! The best way to manage the outcome of the selling process in a nonmanipulative way, focused on the relationship, is to be the chosen expert in your field. When you are well-prepared and believe yourself to be the expert, your customers will, too!

 # BURST INTO ACTION

"At the end of all thought must be action."
—Aldous Huxley

(1) Rate each of your current customers on how they perceive you, from Vendor to Advisor.

(2) For any relationship lower than Consultant, list ways you can build trust so customers see you as more of a trusted Advisor.

(3) To move up to Consultant, increase your knowledge of each customer's situation and recommend some solutions that don't include you.

(4) To move up to Team Member, build more internal relationships in the customer's company. Some people can sign nondisclosures that limit themselves to one client per industry to build trust.

(5) To move up to Partner, invite customers to events at your home. Be open and honest. Show them you want to be a partner. Represent their interests to others.

(6) To move up to Advisor, customize your relationship with each customer. Try to be an outsource or "virtual" part of their company. Be a mentor, an expert not on their payroll. Hire other consultants for them at your expense.

(7) Institute a self-training program with specific goals to increase your competence every month in measurable ways.

(8) To start your relationships at higher levels of trust, work to turn referrals into new customers.

(9) Collect testimonials to attest to the value of your services and products.

HOW TO BUILD RELATIONSHIPS WITH ANYBODY

Rick Crandall

Rick Crandall, PhD, is a speaker, writer, and consultant, specializing in talks and workshops on sales and marketing. He has spoken for *Inc.* magazine, the American Marketing Association, Autodesk, Office Depot, and the American Society for Training and Development. Dr. Crandall has presented well over 1,000 public seminars, given many keynote presentations, and worked with organizations from large law firms to the Air Force.

He is the author or editor of five books on marketing including *1001 Ways to Market Your Services: Even If You Hate to Sell* (1998).

Dr. Crandall is the recipient of an SBA Small Business Award, and is listed in various *Who's Who*s.

Rick Crandall, PhD; Agent: Select Press, PO Box 37, Corte Madera, CA 94976-0037; phone (415) 435-4461; fax (415) 435-4841; e-mail RPCrandall@aol.com.

HOW TO BUILD RELATIONSHIPS WITH ANYBODY

Rick Crandall

"I love selling because it gives me a chance to learn about different types of businesses and meet different types of people, some of whom will buy from me. Essentially, I get paid to make new friends."

—Jack Sweeney, sales consultant

If you're like my sales mentor, Jack, you enjoy selling and view it as an opportunity to build relationships. Most of the chapters in this book talk about building long-term relationships with customers. If you want to be a consultant, team member, partner, or advisor to your customers, you need relationship-building skills.

Most successful salespeople are friendly and have a knack for getting along with others. While some people seem to have a natural ability to get along with people, anyone can learn social skills that foster relationship building.

There is a lot of research-derived information on how to build relationships that has never been discussed in a practical sales context. This chapter will reveal this information for your use.

Later in this chapter, I list a baker's dozen ways to build relationships. After you read them, you may feel like they're nothing more than common sense. However, few people could list 13 different relationship-building techniques. And certainly, the state of relationships in the world suggests that we could all use help. Half of all marriages end in divorce. Many of us haven't made a new friend in the last year. Perhaps common sense isn't as common as we'd like to think.

MAJOR BARRIERS TO RELATIONSHIP BUILDING

Why don't we all have great relationships with customers, prospects, and others in our lives? The first answer is that some of your customers want to keep you at the minimal relationship level of Vendor.

Some Customers Don't Want Relationships

My own bias is toward the value of building relationships with customers and suppliers. However, surveys suggest that about 15–20% of people don't want close relationships with their vendors. For instance, I like to be recognized and greeted in restaurants where I frequently dine. I also enjoy talking to the servers. But some of my friends prefer to remain anonymous at restaurants.

A relationship implies a sense of mutual obligation, if only to acknowledge the other per-

"Today's special is grilled salmon, and my service can be ordered in Aloof, Friendly, or Familiar."

son. Some of your customers do not want any feeling of obligation to you. This may be defensiveness on their part in response to having been exploited by others in past relationships.

Treating everyone in a friendly manner will produce the best results, even when the other person doesn't want a relationship. Be careful about writing others off. Many Driver types (impatient, task-oriented, Type A) may seem unfriendly, but *will* build relationships. Try to get them outside of work and see how they respond.

Customers who definitely don't want a relationship may not be worth your investment. All they typically care about are features and price. You'll be better off dealing with people who want a relationship, even if what they want is one-sided with you doing most of the work.

There's Not Enough Time

A Paradox?
People who are too busy are never too busy to talk about how busy they are!

I'm a Driver-type myself. I understand people who aren't socially oriented. I like people, but to stay connected I need to remind myself that nurturing a relationship is an important "task." If you're task- or data-oriented, give yourself the pleasant job of getting to know people better.

Most people are busy. We feel harried, like we don't have time for an extra minute's conversation. However, a minute is about all the time that's required to add something to a relationship. The person who takes a minute to drop a thank-you note or a clipping is forging connections. A courteous minute of conversation here and there can make the difference between beginning to build relationships and always being an outsider. Which would you rather be?

People Don't Deserve My Friendship

We all should learn to enjoy others for the good they offer, and not be put off by the bad (or annoying). If someone is great except for one bad habit, take them for the good and ignore the bad. If they have crazy political attitudes, or chew tobacco, steer them away from that potential discussion, and save clippings (or collectors tobacco tins!) for them.

Unclear Contracts

One important problem in most relationships is unclear "contracts." Many times we each bring expectations to relationships that are never discussed. In fact, deducing other people's agendas is one of the great sales skills. (And trying to hide your agenda is a real trust killer.)

Be clear with new contacts about your goals for a first meeting. They'll respect you for it. And if they're impatient types, they'll throw you out if you don't get to the point!

Ask them about their ideal relationships with vendors. Very few people do this. They'll be surprised and this will help you advance the relationship. If you reach the consultant level (or higher, as discussed in the last chapter), you'll have to prove to your customers that their long-term success really is more important to you than a short-term sale. There's nothing more convincing here than turning down business and helping them coordinate with someone else who you've already checked out for them. I've called this Santa Claus selling.

You Get the Honey

Like the proverbial bee, you can visit many "flowers," pick up some honey and cross-fertilize them with ideas. You don't have to be bothered by either the individual thorns or the disorderly gardens of your customers.

Santa Claus Selling

If you don't have something appropriate, send people to another source. Remember Kris Kringle in Miracle on 34th Street? People became more loyal Macy's customers when he sent them to other stores. You build great credibility when you point out things you can't do . . . . Good referrals to other sources show customers that you really have their best interests at heart.

—Rick Crandall, *Marketing Your Services: For People Who Hate to Sell*

13 SECRETS TO BUILDING RELATIONSHIPS

Enough on why relationships don't work, Now let's have some common sense (backed up by research) on how to build a relationship with anyone.

1 **Treat people differently to get along equally well.** Several chapters in this book mention personality types like Driver, Influencer, Steady, and Analytical. This personality classification is very popular in the business world. Among psychologists, the accepted major personality variables are somewhat similar. The "Big 5" are Extroversion/Introversion, Neuroticism, Openness to Experience, Agreeableness, and Conscientiousness. These personality traits have been found to be far more comprehensive and psychologically valid than other personality systems.

Whatever personality classification system you prefer, the lesson is to adjust your behavior to match individuals' styles. Type A's, who talk fast, get impatient if you don't get to the point soon enough. Type B's, who like a slower pace, get nervous around Type A's. For instance, if you're a "fast-talking New Yorker," you won't be trusted in the South, and vice versa—at least not on first meeting. If you match your prospect's style, the first meeting will go smoother—and is more likely to lead to a second meeting.

This advice to be a chameleon in terms of matching other people's styles is interpreted differently in old and new selling. It's largely a matter of intentions. If behavioral matching is done to manipulate people, it is part of old selling. If it is done to make people more comfortable, it is part of the "new selling" advocated by this book.

2 **Reinforce others.** Our basic biology makes us respond positively to things that help our

> The greatest ability in business is to get along with others and influence their actions. A chip on the shoulder is too heavy a piece of baggage to carry through life.
>
> —John Hancock

survival. When we're safe, we feel good. When we're in danger, we feel bad. Honest compliments are fine, but flattery is an old-selling way to make people feel good. And most prospects are too wise for simplistic flattery to work.

Prospects reason that the more you've invested in the relationship with them (reinforced them), the less likely you are to abandon them when they need you. Prospects figure that if you're not persistent when you want their business, you may not be around when you have it.

Another way to put this is to give first, before you expect to get anything. As other chapters mention, you have to look for creative opportunities to do things for people that are meaningful to them. That's where the examples about making them heroes with others come in. Or in networking, ask others what would be a good referral for them. This also leads to the next proven psychological principle of relationship building.

3 Look for reciprocity. Relationships are like conversations: People take turns. Relationships are built from a two-way flow of reinforcement. The rhythm of responsiveness between two parties is as important in relationship building as in a conversation. If you don't respond to friendly overtures, you will break the rhythm. If customers don't respond to yours, they may be unhappy about the relationship.

Relationships become more intimate by back-and-forth stages. In order to move the relationship forward, someone has to take a risk and disclose more of themselves, or do more, than

Pacing Is Everything

Whether you're building your business or your social relationships, pacing is important. If you try to go too fast, you offend or scare off the other person. But if you go too slowly, the other person might feel that you don't care.

The best way to pace any relationship is to use a series of gradually more personal approaches. For instance, in retail, you might introduce yourself to the customer. If they introduce themselves back, it is a sign that you can take another step in making the relationship more personal. If they don't, it suggests that they're not yet comfortable with the idea of a closer relationship.

the immediate relationship warrants. In practice, this can be simple. If your conversations start as strictly business, add a more personal comment. Others will respond if they are in tune with you.

A related way to improve relationships is to move to a different locale. If you only see someone in their office, your relationship is one dimensional. Take the initiative to invite them to the local coffee shop, a ball game, or a party. You'll see another side of them and advance the relationship.

> Any fact is better established by two or three good testimonies, than by a thousand arguments.
>
> —Emmons

4 Find similarities in personal or business areas. This is some of the oldest common sense advice, supported by hundred of studies by psychologists such as Donn Byrne. While different people can get along well because they complement each other, research is overwhelming that similarity leads to liking.

People feel safer if you have things in common with them. Especially if you share values, they can understand you better, and predict your decisions. If you share friends in common, you are less likely to exploit them because the word will spread to others. This is why referrals provide extra leverage for you—because they provide extra safety for prospects.

One system of persuasion that is popular—neurolinguistic programming (NLP)— trains you to mirror people in tone, pacing, and body language. This form of similarity could be effective, but there is not much detailed research evidence to support it.

Canned Referrals

If you want to have referrals at your beck and call, collect testimonials and carry them with you.

While written testimonials are the norm, audio and video testimonials can be even more effective. Listening to a customer's voice makes the testimonial more "real" and credible. Get some tapes made and leave them with interested prospects.

---

5 Ask questions and listen more than you talk. (See also Chapter 8 on listening, and Chapters 4 and 5 on asking questions.) One way to reinforce people is to show interest in what they say. For instance, one night I decided to get along with a woman I'd always found to be self-centered and had therefore avoided, even though her husband was a friend and professional contact. I started by asking how she was doing. Then I asked about her music (she played and taught). Then I asked her how her classes were going, and so forth. After the party, on the way home, she mentioned to her husband what a good conversation she'd had with me. In about an hour, I had talked for perhaps five minutes. That's the way to be a great conversationalist with many people!

A cautionary note: Occasionally, I've been asked questions by individuals who have probably been told that this is a good way to get along with people. Sometimes it feels more like a prisoner-of-war interrogation. They ask one question after another, but never give me reciprocal information. Or they launch into a series of questions without either telling me why they're asking, or without getting "permission."

6 **Repeated exposure.** In the 1970s, I was about the fifth most-published expert on the effects of repeated exposure on liking (it was a small area)! We would lock people in rooms and show them stimuli (designs or nonsense words, usually). Some stimuli were shown only a few times, others were shown hundreds of times. While we could make the participants sick of a particular design or nonsense word with too many exposures, a week later, they chose as their favorites the stimuli they had seen the most.

In one experiment, researchers tested the effects of seeing people varying numbers of times. People who had signed up to participate in an experiment were moved around the research rooms such that they "accidently" saw each other a different number of times as they were doing

> One of the best ways to persuade others is with your ears—by listening to them.
> —Dean Rusk

> 90% of success in life is just showing up!
> —Woody Allen

another experiment. In general, the participants most liked the people they saw the most frequently. In other words, the more you see something, the more you like it—and that includes people.

When you stay in contact with people, they will come to like you more, unless you are negatively reinforcing them. This frequency effect can even override the fairly powerful effect of physical attractiveness discussed next.

7 Attractive people are liked more. Unfair as it may be, physically attractive people tend to be liked more. Research has shown that good looks provide benefits in many contexts. For instance, if you're ever arrested, the jury is less likely to find you guilty if you're better looking than average. And physically attractive people are perceived to be more intelligent.

Now, most of us aren't going to invest in plastic surgery to improve our looks. But, we can all dress well and be well groomed.

8 Send "stuff" that interests them. I read a lot, so I frequently come across items about others' interests, companies, or industries. It's relatively easy to pop an article in an envelope and mail it off. Most people appreciate the gesture, primarily because it shows that you're thinking about them, and secondly, because sometimes the material is of value.

I also collect books, so while I'm scouring shops and flea markets for books that interest me, I frequently see books in others' areas of business or personal interest. When Gerald Ford was president, I noticed an ad in an old book for a 1930s' series of books called *The Jerry Ford Wonder Stories.* I sent him a copy of the ad and offered to look for the books for him. He responded with a nice personal note, even though he didn't want me to look for the books for him.

One accountant subscribes to clients' industry publications and has his assistant clip articles of interest to each. This is a way to delegate the finding of personal material. More traditional mailings, such as your company newsletter personalized with a note from you, qualify as weak "stuff." Faxes of cartoons and jokes are also often used. The more you know about each person's interests—personal and business—the easier it will be to find items that hit the mark. This leads to the next item.

9 Be smarter—use a system to keep track of information. First, you have to collect information about your customers and prospects. Then you have to remember it. Fortunately, any of us can be a genius at remembering information by using a database. Even a paper-and-pencil system, reviewed before each contact, can suffice if you're phobic about computers.

A simple example occurred when I took my daughter in for a doctor's appointment. The doctor's first question to my daughter wasn't about symptoms, but rather, "How is Spooky [her cat]?" That one question personalized the interaction for my daughter and put her at ease. And, on the doctor's part, all it took was writing the cat's name on her chart.

10 Balance your life—work all the time! Just kidding. As mentioned in the networking chapter, leisure set-

Hot Topics

Make notes on what different individuals enjoy talking about. Then, whenever possible, offer them new information on that topic.

For example, some people enjoy industry gossip—who's jumping to a new company, who landed a big contract, and so forth. Other people might enjoy talking about restaurants. Start your conversation out on the person's topic of interest. When you learn new information, it gives you a nonsales reason to call and further the relationship.

A topic many people enjoy talking about more than themselves is their children. (Hint: When you note children's ages in your database, do it by year of birth or in relation to your own child's age, for example, "2 years older than Sue." That will avoid your making any embarrassing comments from an old note about "9-year-old Billy" who is now 13.)

Database Success

Bill Clinton started keeping notes on contacts when he was in college. By 1980, his contact file had grown to 10,000 names. He later got the names into a computer database file, so he was better able to keep track of his interactions with each contact.

tings are a great place to build relationships. You already start with a common interest. One lawyer who rides mountain bikes met one of his biggest clients while biking. The client owned a mountain bike company and the fact that the lawyer knew a lot about the product made it easier for them to work together.

Most of us have been meaning to do more leisure activities. If you schedule leisure activities where you can meet other people, it can pay off in business contacts. Meanwhile, you'll be balancing your life, so you enjoy yourself whether you make great contacts or not.

11 **Go new places.** If you had to make a new friend in the next week, you might have a hard time of it. If you always go the same places, you'll always meet the same people.

If you join your customers' trade groups, it's not unlikely that you will be the only person from your industry. In most groups, members volunteer to recruit new members. Groups always need new members, and most people aren't keen on calling on strangers! But you have that skill, and selling is even easier when you're selling for a nonprofit group.

One insurance agent volunteered to be on the membership committee for his customer's trade group. When he recruits people for the group, he makes it a policy not to talk about his business.

When new recruits attend their first meeting, he acts as host and introduces them to other members. He's a star in the group, and a friend to new members. He gets a lot of business from group members—people call him because he is liked, and is perceived as responsible and a go-getter.

12 **Show a sense of hu-mor.** Research shows that people like people who have a sense of humor. Having a sense of humor doesn't mean you have to tell jokes. It means you aren't grim about life. You have a wry way of looking at the world and

> ## Good Relationships Multiply
>
> If you build good, solid connections, when buyers at any of your accounts leave, they'll bring you in as a supplier at their new companies.

yourself. You use a little self-deprecating humor, especially if you're high status. People feel better after being around you, not worse. So spread a little cheer today. Research shows it's contagious!

13 **Be yourself.** Much of the popular litera-ture on how to find a mate, make friends, and influence people recommends doing things that don't match the "real you." In my seminars, I've argued that if you attract people by being what you're not—phoney—it won't be much of a relationship.

Many times we complain that people don't know the real us. Who's fault is that? Your customers and your friends can't read minds. In order to start the positive reciprocity of point 3 above, it's up to you to reveal something about yourself to others. What we're talking about here is sincerity. There's a cynical saying in old-style selling that if you can fake sincerity, you've got it made! But, if you're not sincere, people generally know it. By revealing little things about yourself that don't make you look perfect, you come across as a normal person with normal flaws, and you show your sincerity.

A CULTURE OF RELATIONSHIPS

I've talked with many overseas companies about doing business in the U.S. A stereotype exists that Japanese and European companies are much more concerned about long-term relationships than their American counterparts.

While it's certainly true that without relationships, U.S. companies are at a disadvantage overseas, I think that the actual picture is more complex than the stereotype. Many foreign nationals are struck by how "superficial" Americans' friendliness is. I believe it's just that it's much easier to start relationships in the U.S., but just as hard to build strong ones. Americans tend to be more friendly and open with strangers. We are informal and reach first-name status faster. That can give the impression of more intimacy than really exists.

This concept of superficial friendliness is also the image of the old-style sales pro—Willie Loman with a back slap and a smile. While skill in making a friendly first impression is still valuable, you'll be better off having deeper connections and less glad handing.

To practice "new selling," you have to be capable of building relationships. While relationship skills are usually considered an art, they are actually a science. Some people are born with an inclination towards skills that help in sales, but we can all learn to get along better with others.

If you think you're already applying all these skills, keep track of one a day. I'll bet you find areas to improve. I know I do.

> A salesman is somebody way up there in the blue, riding on a smile and a shoe shine.
> —Willie Loman in Arthur Miller's *Death of a Salesman*

BURST INTO ACTION

"The great purpose of life is not knowledge but action."

—Thomas Huxley

(1) If you don't enjoy the kinds of people in the industries you serve, get out of the business or get an attitude adjustment!

(2) Classify the personalities of your customers

and make notes on how best to get along with each.

(3) Develop ways to discuss the kind of "relation-ship contract" your prospects and customers want.

(4) Create mechanisms such as regular business e-mail to keep in touch with customers when you're not selling to them.

(5) Develop more reasons to be in front of custom-ers so they have more chances to like you.

(6) Meet customers outside of their office environ-ments more frequently.

(7) Implement a system to send items of both business and personal interest.

NEEDS ANALYSIS
Don't Sell,
Help People Buy

Linda M. Keats

Linda M. Keats is the president and cofounder of The Corporate Training Group, Inc. Speaker, trainer, and professional consultant, Mrs. Keats has over 23 years of experience in sales and sales management. Most recently, she has been responsible for developing training programs, telephone scripts, marketing programs, sales presentations, and workshops designed to provide maximum results utilizing advanced selling, communication, and negotiation principles for today's marketplace.

Current workshops include: Prospecting into the 21st Century™, The Virtual Sales Professional™, Telesales, Ambassador Client Servicing, Coaching and Leadership for Managers and Supervisors, Time Management, Goal Setting, and Personality Styles Identification and Adaptation for the Sales Professional.

Mrs. Keats' list of clients includes Royal & Sun Alliance, Panasonic, BellSouth, The Prudential, Allstate, and Home Depot, to name just a few. She has spoken nationally for Life and Health Underwriters associations, The Association of Professional Saleswomen, The American Society for Training and Development, The International Customer Service Association, and Sales and Marketing Executives International. Currently, Mrs. Keats is active in ASTD, SMEI, and GEWN.

Linda M. Keats, The Corporate Training Group, Inc., 3610 Dekalb Tech. Pkwy. #106, Atlanta, GA 30340; phone (770) 986-6190; fax (770) 986-6192; e-mail ctg@ctginet.com.

NEEDS ANALYSIS
Don't Sell,
Help People Buy

Linda M. Keats

"Seek first to understand, then to be understood."
—Stephen Covey

Despite continuing change, one thing in business remains constant: *Nothing happens until someone sells something!*

CLASSIC "OLD-STYLE" SELLING

We have all heard that there is not much new in selling, and for the most part, that is true. Most sales professionals still use the "thank you for meeting with me today, let me tell you why you should be doing business with us" approach. Although this show-and-tell presentation style is polished and attempts to engage the customer to some degree, the sales professional, not the *customer*, remains the primary focus.

Some of the problems facing sales profession-als are actually of their own doing. Many sales professionals consider their approaches consulta-tive, but closer examination often reveals a rather price-oriented, commodity-focused and, therefore, ineffective "nonconsultative" sales process.

SELLING ON PRICE

Price-oriented selling is characterized by such offers as, "Where do I need to be to get the sale?" or "Tell me what the competitor is offering, and I'll see what I can do to match it."

If you're not comfortable selling the value of your products and services, then price becomes the key selling point. There are many dangers to selling on price. When you are willing to drop on price without conversation, your customer will assume your prices were inflated from the outset. This immediately lessens your credibility. And, after dropping your price so quickly once, you become an easy target for ongoing discounting pressure.

Selling on price also allows the customer to consider price against his or her own percep-tions of value. It is too late to attempt to sell the value of your product or service after the customer's mind is made up. (See also Chapter 6 on selling value.) Closing on price, asking for the order, getting an objection, and then selling value to overcome the objection is selling in reverse. With this reverse process, customers do not ap-preciate what they are paying for, so when you close on price they "fill in the blanks" with their own perceptions of value.

Dealing with Price

Here are two re-sponses used by sales pros when people ask for a lower price. One is to ask if they sell for the lowest price; and when they say, no, ask them, "Why not?" Then after they ex-plain, you say, "Me, too." An-other is to say, "I'm sure our competitors know the value of their services better than we do!"

—Rick Crandall, *1001 Ways to Market Your Services: Even If You Hate to Sell*

Some sales professionals who attempt to sell on price still fail to close the sale because they lose the business to a competitor with the relationship advantage. Selling on price builds no relationship. It leaves the sales professional vulnerable to the customer moving his or her business elsewhere as soon as a better deal comes along. Building relationship value with your customers overcomes this problem. You must create a relationship with your customers so that they feel more comfortable with you than with any of the competitors . . . regardless of price.

"NEW" SELLING

For the last ten or so years, we have begun hearing about a concept known as Consultative Selling. While often used in a generic sense of acting as a consultant for the customer, in fact, this term is almost 30 years old and trademarked!* Some other customer-oriented sales processes are known as: Solution Selling, Strategic Selling, and Integrity Selling.

There are many ways to be customer-oriented in selling. What all techniques should have in common is helping customers find out what they need, and then offering your products and services as solutions to those needs—*when appropriate.*

Advantages of Helping People Buy

The benefits of using customer-oriented selling should be obvious:

- There is more customer involvement.
- You can match the customer's needs to certain of your products and services.
- A relationship of trust is built.
- You don't have to hard sell.
- There will be less resistance when buying.

*Mack Hanan, *Consultative Selling* (AMACOM Books)

- There will be overall increased customer satisfaction due to your concentration on specifically identified needs.
- There will be more profitable repeat business and referrals.

This new sales philosophy has turned the "used-car salesman" image of trickery, high pressure, and manipulation to induce a sale upside down. The new terminology and customer-focused sales principles have helped change perceptions about the sales profession.

Just What Exactly Is "New" Selling?

In true New Selling, customers do most of the talking, and the sales professional most of the listening. Effective selling offers a seamless and specific sales sequence, integrating communication, relationship building, and negotiation so smoothly that customers move willingly through the process to make many purchases over time.

"Hello, Daily News. Delete the word 'aggressive' from our ad for salespeople. Replace it with 'friendly and helpful.'"

New Selling makes customers the primary beneficiaries of the sales process. Customers no longer see the salesperson as someone sitting on the opposite side of the table, trying to talk them out of their money. Now customers see the salesperson as a necessary extension of a business, someone with the skill and the knowledge to offer real and valuable business solutions.

THE NEW SALES MODEL

To help customers buy, the sales professional—you—must get the buyer to discuss the value elements he or she is willing to invest in. This requires communication skills and the ability to conduct a thorough Needs Analysis. When there is a fit, you can then position your offerings as the solutions the customer has been looking for. Suddenly, price becomes secondary.

The focus here is on allowing the customer to do the majority of the talking. This gives you the opportunity to gather all the information you need to assure the customer that you have answers to his or her needs. Very little time is spent in the closing portion of the sales process because objections have already been confronted and dealt with earlier. The close is merely the natural end to a satisfying process for customer and sales professional alike.

The New Sales Model, as I use it, is composed of The Virtual Presenter, The Virtual Communicator and The Virtual Sales Technician. Successful New Selling requires mastery of each of these.

The Virtual Presenter

As a sales professional, you are in charge of moving your customer relationships forward. In the old-style selling, that would involve efforts at control. In New Selling, it involves questions and needs analysis.

The Virtual Communicator

A sales professional can be a wizard with industry knowledge and expertise, and still be an ineffective salesperson due to a lack of communication skills.

Effective communication is made possible by five equally critical elements:

- **listening** (the ability and the discipline to hear and interpret both words and meanings (also see Chapter 8)
- **verbal skill** (delivery, word selection, and tone of voice)

The New Sales Model

- **nonverbal communication** (body language and eye contact)
- **feedback** (to ensure clarity of understanding)
- **style adaptation** (understanding the four social styles and their preferred modes of communication)

Sales is a people business. People will do more business with those with whom they are *most* comfortable. Achieving this level of relationship through the use of effective communication allows the sales professional to change customers' perceptions of value, investment, cost, and benefits. This change in customers' perceptions will lead to a change in their buying behavior. Your customers will reward your having made them feel comfortable with increased customer loyalty and diminished sensitivity to price.

Consider your customer relationships and ask yourself the following questions:

- Have your customers told you they prefer to do business with you over your competitors?
- Have you witnessed horizontal growth and relationship development within existing accounts?
- Have you observed increased customer retention and less price sensitivity?
- How about increased tolerance and willingness to work through problems and differences?

Create a plan to improve your communication skills so you can foster your consultative behavior.

Now, let's move on to the other piece of The New Sales Model, The Virtual Sales Technician.

The Virtual Sales Technician

NEEDS ANALYSIS
✔ Ask
✔ Listen
✔ Provide

To complete the sales process, the communication skills discussed above must be complemented by sales tools deliberately sequenced to move a customer willingly and naturally through the sales process.

This is where you put a Needs Analysis model of **Ask**, **Listen**, and **Provide** to good use. With strong communication skills, you will not want to "preach" at your customers and prospects. Rather, spend time right from the start asking questions to understand their needs.

When it comes time for the presentation, avoid canned approaches. These will not be effective because they address only the points the salesperson has memorized. Not all customers have the same needs, so your sales presentation must be adjusted to each customer's social style, needs, and the scenario at hand. (See also Chapter 10 on presentations.)

THE NEEDS ANALYSIS

While each component of the relationship-building and sales process is important, let's take a closer look at conducting an effective Needs Analysis. This is your opportunity—as a sales professional—to gain insight into the wants and needs of your customers, and to allay their anxieties before they have a chance to develop into problems. Therefore, the Needs Analysis is the most critical part of your sales process.

A Needs Analysis should include:

- buyer need for your products and services and ability to pay (qualifying)
- questions that uncover motives or concerns
- needs-based questions
- thought-provoking questions
- discussion about how the customer has previously used companies like yours, and his or her current situation
- discussion of the customer's decision-making process and time frame
- uncovering of any necessary statistical, demographic, or technical information
- uncovering any negative issues or concerns, and the resolutions needed

This is the time for the customer to speak and the sales professional to listen and take notes.

Checklist Selling

In some cases, needs analysis can also be done through written questions.

For example, one successful insurance agent has trained thousands of others to use about 80 brief questions covering financial situations. These multiple-choice questions can be answered in about nine minutes. The questions help people understand their own needs, demonstrate the agent's expertise and establish him as a consultant, qualify people, and guide the potential sales conversation. If the answers aren't "right," there is no sales effort.

Questions

Notice that much of a Needs Analysis consists of questions. Questions are an invaluable sales tool. They may be used throughout a sales presentation, but are especially important in the introductory segment. The sequence of the questions is perhaps more important than the types of questions themselves. It is the sequence that positions the sale and offers "momentum" by creating interest in the customer's mind.

The five types of sequenced questions I use are: (1) general; (2) directional; (3) needs, wants, and concerns; (4) focusing; and (5) target. (See the box below for an explanation of how the questions are used.)

It is important to use open-ended questions (those questions which solicit information) rather than close-ended questions which only solicit yes or no responses. Open-ended questions allow customers to elaborate what is important to them. Use the customer's words and meanings to determine the best possible targeted sales approach. Open-ended questions typically begin with: who, what, why, where, when, how, describe, share, explain, and review.

To compose your questions, think in reverse of the *ask* sequence, beginning with the ultimate: What is your goal (target)? Where do you want to end up at the end of this meeting or process? Then, think about what questions will help you to understand the customer's sales and decision-making process (focusing). What questions will expose the customer's needs, wants, or concerns (needs)? What questions will assess the customer's current circumstances (direc-

Needs Analysis Questions

1 **General questions** are used to "warm up" the customer and keep the salesperson from jumping ahead to the bottom line.

2 **Directional questions** then focus the conversation toward clarifying and assessing the customer's unique circumstances.

3 **Needs, wants, and concerns questions** next expose the customer's "hot buttons" and "smoke out" concerns, allowing the sales professional to eliminate potential objections.

4 **Focusing questions** move the customer into position for action by uncovering his or her decision-making process.

5 **Target questions** tell the salesperson exactly what he or she needs to do to obtain the business or successfully reach the next step in the sales process.

Sample Needs Analysis Questions for a First Meeting with a Prospective Customer

Here are some sample questions as examples of those you might use:

General questions

- How many years have you been with the company and what is your area of responsibility?
- What is your relationship to the _____ process?
- Who in your department, other than yourself, will be involved in the _____ process?
- What is your time frame for making a decision?

Directional questions

- Which _____ companies have you worked with in the past and how were these companies selected?
- How did these companies respond when any problems occurred and what was your overall satisfaction with their responses?
- What kind of measurement was used to assess their impact on your company?
- How well have they performed against these measurements?

Needs, wants, and concerns questions

- If you could create the ideal relationship with a _____ company, what would you like to see?
- If you could name two or three valuable services a _____ company should provide, what would they be and why?

- What kind of valuable solutions has your current company offered you and how have these solutions impacted your bottom line?
- What do you like about your current _____ company and on what things would you like to see improvement?

Focusing questions

- What is your budget for_____?
- How often do you review proposals?
- What will you be looking for in a proposal in order to consider a company?
- How open will you be to allowing us to review competing proposals to offer a line-by-line comparison?

Target questions

- What would you need to see or hear from us in order to select our company as your _____ supplier?
- Under what circumstances would we be eliminated from consideration?
- If we are able to provide your company with improved _____ and enhanced _____ along with increased _____ will you consider our service?
- Should you like what you hear today, what would you say our next step should be?

tional)? Finally, decide on those questions that will reveal information about the customer's company or personal circumstances or responsibilities (general).

All customers have key issues, wants, and needs. Your goal through an effective Needs Analysis is to help customers clarify their critical issues, wants, and needs so you can adapt your offerings to help in those specific areas. Consider what your customers want and are willing to pay for. Then convert these issues, wants, and needs into effective questions and assemble them into a sequence to form a conversational dialogue.

Business Issues and Solutions Your Customers Want and Would Be Willing to Pay For

- enhanced productivity
- reduced costs
- improved customer retention
- increased growth
- greater simplicity
- greater versatility
- enhanced reliability
- increased value
- improved technology
- increased responsiveness
- increased efficiency
- ease of use
- time savings
- reduced risk
- increased convenience
- reduced turnover
- improved customer image

Think of possible questions for these business issues that apply to what you offer. Use them to draw out customers' issues, wants, and needs. You'll better understand what they will need from you in order to be comfortable doing business with you.

EIGHT KEYS TO ASKING QUESTIONS

1 **In selecting your key questions, always consider:**
- your goal
- your customer's position on the "food chain"
- the social style of the customer

2 **Develop a different needs analysis model and set of questions for each of your primary types of meetings and presentations.** You can use these models as you prepare for a meeting by customizing the series of questions to correspond with the customer scenario. This will greatly expedite the learning curve of using the Needs Analysis process.

3 **Always be prepared to eliminate questions.** At times, the customer has a different need or agenda from that which you have prepared. You are offering a customer-based presentation format, and so will need to be flexible.

4 **Use questions to close any "loopholes" your customers use in their answers.** Avoid "skimming" over their answers simply to get to the next question. Listen to their responses and consider additional questions that could dig even deeper to fully understand any insight the customer may have to offer.

5 **Use questions as a guide only.** Have a real conversation. Sometimes you may use all of your questions, but other times you may use only some of your prepared questions. This will be determined by the customer's answers.

6 **Listen and take notes to help keep you focused—be a consultant rather than a salesperson.** Remember, you are asking the questions to learn the needs and concerns of your customer.

7 **Be prepared for unexpected answers to your questions.** Prepare additional questions for the different answers.

8 **Do not sell until all of your necessary questions have been addressed in sequence.** Selling prematurely can create an objection or cause you to forget to go back to the additional questions that would help you further explore any "openings" or needs.

A Cooler Analysis Strategy

A Trane Air Conditioning salesperson focused on multimillion-dollar sales for large buildings. It was hard to distinguish the Trane product from competitors.

The salesperson developed a 40-point questionnaire. He offered to conduct a study for prospects to advise them what type of system would be best for their buildings. He charged $750—a low cost compared to a million-dollar sale.

The needs analysis gave the salesperson a foot in the door and helped build the relationship with prospects. He got most of the later business.

—Donald H. Sandler and John Hayes,
*You Can't Teach a Kid to Ride a Bike
at a Seminar*

Sample Needs Analysis Conversation

This conversation exemplifies the use of Directional, and Needs, Wants, and Concerns questions. Target and Focusing questions should be used to close the conversation.

SP = Sales Professional; C = Customer

SP: I understand that your company has been using widgets manufactured by the Acme company. How long have you been using them?

C: They've been our primary supplier for the last fifteen years now.

SP: I noticed you said primary supplier—do you have more than one supplier?

C: We use two additional suppliers as backups. They also provide additional services.

SP: What kind of additional services?

C: Maintenance of our local facilities.

SP: Going back to Acme—what was the original reason for going with them fifteen years ago?

C: They were the first company to come around before our expansion. They have been extremely supportive in our growth and have helped facilitate the building of our new plant.

SP: What specifically would you say are their strengths?

C: Responsiveness and innovation.

SP: What do you mean by responsiveness?

C: They are quick to respond when there is a problem and will take immediate action to correct a mistake—no questions asked.

SP: What about their service offers innovation?

C: They offered suggestions for our new facility that amounted to a reduction in costs to produce our finished products.

SP: Why do you feel that responsiveness and innovation are the most important factors to consider when selecting a widget company as a supplier?

C: In today's marketplace we need every possible advantage.

SP: Other than what we have discussed and being price competitive, what are some of the other factors that are important to your business?

C: Track record and experience in our industry. We want a company to fully understand our business.

SP: How would you describe your ideal relationship with a supplier?

C: Ease of use, prompt service, open communication, superior quality, and competitive pricing.

SP: Let's discuss each of these points: How would you describe ease of use? . . . What is prompt service? . . . What is open communication? . . . What is superior quality? . . . What are you looking for in a competitive pricing arrangement? (Ask the customer for examples.)

C: Ease of use means . . . prompt service is . . . open communication is . . . (etc.)

SP: What kind of online capabilities have suppliers offered to automate your ordering process and statusing process for all outstanding orders?

C: We have been talking about that, but we haven't done anything yet.

SP: In what way would you say your company would benefit most from implementing an online system for ordering and statusing?

C: We could reduce the amount of paper processing and possibly move two or three full-timers over to another department.

WHERE TO GO FROM HERE?

As is true for the delivery of the entire sales presentation, the Needs Analysis cannot be made up of a canned set of questions. Rather, it is a model of prepared questions that will be used as a conversational guide to help steer the conversation towards the ultimate goal. The majority may be the same from one customer to the next, but the questions must be customized to each individual interaction. An effective sales professional must always be ready to respond to the unanticipated customer response.

Practice Makes Perfect

You will want to practice using questions as a consultative business tool for properly understanding your customers' needs. Questions also keep you focused on offering the most appropriate solutions.

It will take some experience to be able to benefit from your prepared models of questions. Once you're comfortable with them, they will successfully help keep you focused to listen to the customers' responses and consider additional questions to better understand each customer. Take notes, truly listening from the customers' perspective to understand how to work *with* customers, rather than sell *to* them.

Prepare some Needs Analysis models to take on your appointments and use as guides. Once you have memorized the questions in their proper sequence, you can discard the models. Remember, all good con-

A Needs Analysis Brochure

As part of their switch from a transactional to a relationship focus, KeyCorp Bank in Cleveland created a brochure called "Retirement Reality Check."

The brochure uses 26 yes-no questions on financing one's retirement. Customers can pick it up at any of 1000 centers. By filling it out, customers end up with a fuller understanding of their needs. KeyCorp then produces a retirement plan that doesn't include product recommendations. This further builds the consultative relationship and leads to new business.

Prescription without diagnosis is malpractice, whether you're a doctor or a salesperson!

sultants ask a lot of questions and take notes before offering their opinions and solutions.

With the information gained from the Needs Analysis, you can customize the rest of your sales process to support or confirm what has already been discussed. You can begin to see that each segment of the whole sales relationship is dependent on a good Needs Analysis. The consultative sales process is like a well-choreographed dance; every piece fits into place, and in the end, the performance is appreciated by both the partners.

SUMMARY

In conclusion, true selling requires you to set aside the ultimate goal of closing the deal. Instead, shift priority to the customer's needs. Customers will want to listen to the solutions you offer when they trust your relationships with them.

Use effective communication skills to build relationships with customers—strong relationships will get you beyond the typical competitive threats like price and look-alike products and services. If you can change a customer's perceptions to seeing you as a trusted problem solver, you will change his or her buying behaviors.

When a deliberate sales process is used in accordance with each customer's preferred communication style, buying situation, and need, you will have a permanent platform on which to position your product and service solutions.

Consultative-type selling demands planning and practice. It is much easier to talk *at* a customer with a memorized and rehearsed spiel. Talking *with* a customer, using communication skills and a customized sales message, takes much more skill and discipline. But it offers the customer the very best solution available—the one you customized to their needs.

It's time for you to get to work. Take a personal-selling inventory by videotaping a typical customer interaction. Consider your current sales process and assess your current style of communication. Then use the information in this book to help redesign your sales approach so that you become a true consultative sales professional. All that's left for you to do, then, is watch as your customer relationships improve and your sales volume increases! Get to it—at this very moment there are customers just waiting to buy!

BURST INTO ACTION

"Unused talents give you no advantage over someone who has no talents at all."
—Mark Twain

(1) Create a plan to improve your personal communication skills. In what areas do you need to improve: listening, verbal skills, nonverbal communication, feedback, or matching others' personal styles?

(2) Analyze your key accounts and develop a plan to strengthen each of these relationships.

(3) Talk with customers with whom you have really good relationships. Ask them what they like and dislike about you and your competitors.

(4) Develop a checklist or questionnaire that customers can answer to clarify their needs—or you can use it as an assessment tool.

(5) Create a list of General questions that help establish rapport.

(6) Create a list of Directional questions that clarify customers' situations.

(7) Create Needs Analysis questions to understand why the customer would act.

SELL BY ASKING QUESTIONS

Joachim de Posada

Joachim de Posada is an international business speaker specializing in sales management, leadership, and team building. Fluent in both English and Spanish, he has worked with clients in more than 20 countries. His clients include 3M, Union Carbide, Citibank, Medtronic, Kodak, Continental Airlines, SmithKline-Beecham, and System One.

His past experience includes sales director of the Learning Systems Division of Xerox Corporation. There, Dr. de Posada participated in the development of consultative selling systems.

His motivational methods have been so successful that they have been transferred to the sports world. He has been a consultant for the NBA's Milwaukee Bucks, Puerto Rican professional teams, and more recently has been involved with the Los Angeles Lakers and the Panamanian Olympic team.

Dr. de Posada is also an adjunct professor at the University of Miami where he created the curriculum for the University's Sales Institute.

A featured television and radio speaker on performance issues, his combination of academia, corporate, and sports gives Dr. de Posada a unique perspective in motivating and inspiring people to new levels of excellence.

Joachim de Posada, Dr. Joachim de Posada and Associates, Inc., 1111 South West 92nd Avenue, Miami, FL 33174; phone (305) 889-4689; fax (305) 229-3008; e-mail JoachimNSA@aol.com

SELL BY ASKING QUESTIONS

Joachim de Posada

"The important thing is not to stop questioning."
—Albert Einstein

Because I grew up in Cuba, everyone asks me if I have ever met Fidel Castro. I have. Let me tell you the story. It illustrates how *not* to sell.

A few days after Castro came to power in 1959, I went to the store with my grandmother and my best friend Tito. In that Walgreen store, I saw a Castro cap. My friend and I decided that we wanted it, so we asked my grandmother to buy it for us. Bless her soul, she would say yes to anything we would ask from her, although she did say, "Joachim, don't you think you might get in trouble with your dad if he sees you with that cap?" I said, "Don't worry, Grandma, I will handle it."

I went back home to have lunch. Shortly after, my father arrived from work. He saw me with my cap on and he said to me, "If I ever see you with that Communist cap again, I will tear your head off." He said it so forcefully that I didn't dare to argue the point. I only said, "I'm sorry, Dad," and tucked my cap away in my back right pocket.

That afternoon, I went to play with Tito at his house. Tito's father was the Argentinian ambassador to Cuba. As we played in the embassy, we observed a lot of people setting tables, moving furniture, carrying cases of liquor, and so forth. Curious, we asked the ambassador what was going on.

He said that the Argentinian government was going to recognize the Castro government as the legitimate government of Cuba and there was to be a party to celebrate the occasion. My friend asked his dad if the both of us could attend the party. His father explained that it was a party for adults only. Then Tito asked, "Well, can we at least stay in the kitchen?" The ambassador said, "All right, but you cannot come out and bother the guests. Is that clear?" We both said "Yes!"

That night, in the kitchen, we climbed on top of a table and peered out the window at the arriving guests. Earl Smith, the American ambassador to Cuba, was at the party, as were many government dignitaries, members of the press, socialites and, also, my parents.

All of a sudden, there was a commotion as people surged towards the front door. We saw Castro and his bodyguards enter the embassy. Much to our amazement, instead of stopping to say hello to the guests and all the VIPs, he came straight to the kitchen to say hello to the cooks, helpers, servants, and other kitchen personnel.

Castro's Poor Marketing Efforts

Suddenly, Castro spotted my friend and me and he walked over to us. "What is your name?" he asked me. I replied, "My name is Joachim de Posada." Castro said, "Oh, I know your father." (He hated my father.) He turned to my friend and asked him the same question. When my friend replied, Castro said, "Oh, you are the ambassador's son."

At that moment, Castro decided that it would be good publicity to have his picture taken with kids. He told us that he wanted a picture with us. As he turned me around, he spotted my Revolution cap in my back pocket and said, "Joachim, you have a Revolution cap. Put it on for the picture." I said, "No, thank you, let's take the picture without the cap." "Come on," he said, "Let's do it with the cap on." I again refused and I told him that my hair would get messed up, that I would rather do it without the cap. I even took the cap out of my pocket and showed it to him, but I sure wasn't going to put that thing on my head and risk the wrath of my father.

By this time, the kitchen was full of people, reporters, photographers, and TV cameramen all watching this kid saying no to Castro. I was getting very nervous. I was only 12, but I was no dummy— I was defying the most powerful man in the country. I was sweating, sort of looking around for help, when I saw my poor father signaling with his hand towards his head, mouthing the words, "Put the cap on." As you can see in the picture, I did put the cap on. Look at my sad face—I knew I was going to be in big trouble when I got home.

A few months later, my sister and I were put on a plane bound for Freedom. My parents were able to escape the Communist dictatorship shortly thereafter and joined us in the United States.

12-year-old Joachim de Posada looks apprehensive after donning his Revolution cap at the insistence of Fidel Castro

What are the sales lessons here? Instead of Castro *telling* me what to do, he should have made me *want* to do it. How could he have made me want to put the cap on?

He should have asked me questions. The most important skill in the world of sales is how to ask good questions. He should have asked me why I didn't want to wear my cap. I was only 12, so I might have told him. Then, he would have had a chance to handle my objection. Or, his questions might have prompted me to put the cap on to avoid the consequences of having to answer him. The point is, he could not sell me by telling me what to do— I only put the cap on after getting the nod from my father.

QUESTIONS SELL

If you can think and ask questions, you can sell. I am amazed at the number of sales lost because the salesperson doesn't know how to ask questions. What most salespeople know how to do—are even taught to do—is simply to recite the features of the product or service. We call that, *spraying and praying*. They recite all the features to see if one sticks, hoping the prospect likes something and then buys. In today's competitive world, talking features simply doesn't cut it.

> The wise man doesn't give the right answers, he poses the right questions.
> —Claude Levi-Strauss

Understand this: At the beginning of a sales interaction, prospects don't believe you and might not even like you, so anything you say will not be believed. There is no point in *telling* them anything because trust hasn't been established yet. You haven't earned it.

Start earning trust by showing a real interest in, and concern for, your prospect. Ask the right kind of questions so that you can start identifying problems or areas of need, as discussed in the last chapter. This is what we teach to our *Fortune 500* clients. Simple, but, in reality, difficult to do. It takes hours of instruction and practice.

SELLING FROM A BEGINNER'S STATE OF MIND

Selling is one of the few professions where the score card is kept daily. An insurance company found that, for its newly hired salespeople, sales would gradually increase for the first 18 months.

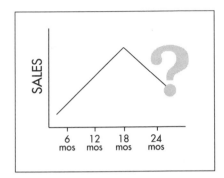

Then, however, sales would start declining. Management was perplexed and proposed all kinds of theories about why this was happening. The most popular explanation was that the salespeople would run out of family members and friends!

The answer turned out to be experience! After much research, they discovered that after 18 months the salespeople would reach a high level of knowledge and considered themselves experts in insurance. At the beginning, the salespeople didn't know that much about insurance and they asked a lot of questions of their prospects. The new agents were, in fact, doing it the right way: asking questions first and then satisfying needs with products.

As "experts," the salespeople felt they knew what the prospects needed and started telling instead of selling. When they stopped asking questions, sales went down.

In sales, you must have an attitude of a learner instead of an attitude of an expert. People, by nature, like to prove experts wrong, to know more than the experts do. Your attitude should be one of wanting to learn and wanting to share something instead of trying to prove you know something your prospects don't. Learn this lesson now, and your sales will increase.

> Learn as though you would never be able to master it.
> —Confucius

Diagnosis First

Discover problems before you sell solutions, not the other way around. This is consultative selling™. This is relationship selling. It is not pushing products or services in order to make a sale and a commission. It is not reciting features to see what sticks (spray and pray). It is taking your customers' interests to heart and really helping them find solutions to their problems.

How do you do this? By asking questions. This is such an important skill—in fact, the most important skill in sales—that it is the focus of this chapter. See the box to the right for examples of questions.

SALES THROUGH QUESTIONS: TWO RESEARCH PATHS CONVERGE

When I was with Xerox, we knew the importance of questioning skills and we made sure that we taught them to our salespeople all over the world. I started with Xerox in 1971 and, by 1979, I had become manager of sales training for the U.S. and Canada for Xerox Learning Systems.

In 1979, Xerox was in trouble. Our market share had fallen from approximately 75% to barely 13%. We had allowed the Japanese to pull the rug out from under our feet. Xerox decided to reinvent itself. We installed a total quality management system so that our products would be built more effectively and with better quality at a lower cost. We reinvented the company, going from a copier-duplicator company to a document company. And, of course, we had to make sure that we had the best-trained sales force in the world.

A State-of-the-Art Sales Training Program

To that end, we were developing a sales course called Account Development Strategies that was going to be the state of the art in sales training. It covered how to develop accounts; how to ask the

---

Open Relationship Doors with Open-Ended Questions

You already know that there are two kinds of questions: open- and closed-ended. Open-ended questions are those that allow the prospect to talk—they can't be answered with a simple "yes" or "no." Questions such as:

- What is it that you do?
- What areas do you cover?
- Why do you do it that way?
- What other things should you consider?
- How?
- Tell me more!
- Where is the problem?
- When is the best time to do such and such?

As you can see, these questions allow the prospect to talk.

Account Development Strategies™

SPIN™ Selling

right questions; how to determine who the decision maker is and who the influencers are; how to determine the organizational needs, the company and the personal needs of the decision makers—even how to overcome obstacles. A very complete course indeed.

A Program Better Than Ours?

Then, out of the blue, came a call from our person in London who told us that they had a psychologist who had the best sales course in the world! We told him to forget it, that we had just finished testing Account Development Strategies, that ours was the best course in the world and they would be receiving it within a month. He said it was too late, that they had already hired the man.

Why did they do that, we asked? The fellow in London said the psychologist had told Xerox to send him to their worst territory—if my memory serves me right, it was South Africa—and that he would turn it into the most productive territory. He went there and he took it to the top in sales. We told London to send this wonderful sales trainer to see us in the U.S.

Questions Unite Us

One Saturday morning in 1979, we in Xerox Learning Systems met with this sales trainer. His name was Neil Rackham. When he started explaining his system, our jaws slowly dropped. We had collected data from thousands of sales calls. He had analyzed over 35,000 sales calls and he had reached the same conclusion that we had. We both came up with the same fundamental finding: There were many more questions asked in successful calls—those leading to advances in the sale or actual orders—than in unsuccessful ones.

Asking questions was the most important skill in sales. Two continents apart, with separate research, we had reached the same conclusion. Validation in its purest form.

SPIN™ SELLING

Let me explain the question-based selling system using Dr. Rackham's terminology.

You ask open-ended and closed-ended questions, but in a certain way. You ask the questions in a sequence that will give you information to develop key questions. These questions cause the customer to come up with the problems that you, the salesperson, will solve.

There are four kinds of questions. The sequence in which they are asked determines your success in advancing the sale. The acronym SPIN gives you the type of questions and the order:

- **S**ituation
- **P**roblem
- **I**mplication
- **N**eed-payoff

Situation Questions

These are questions to assess the situation—what the facts are, what they are doing now, and how are they doing it. In this phase, you find out everything you can about the business so that you can identify problem areas.

Some examples of Situation questions:
- What is your business?
- How many employees do you have?
- How do you take care of distribution?
- How many years in business?

Rackham says, "In calls that succeed, sellers ask fewer Situation questions than in calls that fail." Why? Because when you're making serious

When a salesperson . . . wants me to teach them basic facts about our business, I get irritated. In today's world, I'm too busy for that. I don't get much value from educating salespeople.
—Purchasing VP cited in *The SPIN Selling Field Book*

Do Your Homework

Go on sales calls well prepared. Investigate the company:

- Who are they?
- What do they do?
- Who do they do business with?
- Who are competitors?
- Who are their employees?
- How do they interact with the community?
- Who do they owe money to?
- Do they have an Internet Web site? If they do, visit it and get as much information as you can.
- Who are you dealing with?
- Is he or she the decision maker?

sales calls on big prospects, you're supposed to have already done your homework and learned about their situations. So you'll need fewer Situation questions than if you had gone in cold.

Problem Questions

These questions are designed to pinpoint problems. You should already know quite a bit about your prospect from your Situation questions and any pre-call investigation. You know which problems the customer might have, so you know what questions to ask. Some examples of Problem questions are:

- Are you having delays in your deliveries?
- Do you have problems in meeting the schedule?
- How much waste do you have now?
- Having untrained salespeople—how is it affecting your sales?

Implications are the language of decision makers, and if you can talk their language, you'll influence them better.

—Neil Rackham,
SPIN Selling

Implication Questions

These questions ask about the consequences or effects of buyers' problems. Some examples of Implication questions are:

- If your deliveries are delayed, how does that affect your relationship with your customers?
- How does it affect your accounts receivables?
- What happens if the customers tell other prospects?

Need-Payoff Questions

These are the happy questions. These questions ask if there is an interest in solving the problem that by now is very big after you have asked your Problem and Implication questions. These questions determine if you really have discovered a need that you can now satisfy with a benefit of your product or service. Some examples of Need-Payoff questions are:

- Would you be interested in being able to deliver on-time every time?
- Would it be important to you to find a way to have your people well trained?
- Would you be interested in a solution to this problem?

The research—from both Xerox and Rackham—established that successful people asked many more Problem and Implication questions than the mediocre or unsuccessful salespeople. There was a correlation between success in sales and the ability to ask good questions.

> You never persuade clients of anything. Clients persuade themselves. Your function is to understand the issues that matter to your clients. You have to feel their problems just the way they feel them. You have to sit on their side of the table and look at issues from their point of view.
>
> —An executive cited in *The SPIN Selling Field Book*

CONCLUSION

Consultative, relationship-oriented selling is perhaps the most misunderstood concept in the business world. We used it loosely in Xerox back in the early 1970s. It implied that by asking a few questions, and uncovering a few needs, the salesperson can become a consultative resource to his or her customer. It simply ain't so.

In *Webster's Dictionary*, "consultative" is defined as "having the privilege to consult." Notice the word "privilege." It is actually a privilege that must be earned by the salesperson. It is not achieved by simply being good looking, walking in, smiling, showing an impressive business card, and becoming a priest or psychologist asking all kinds of questions.

The privilege is earned by using the skills taught in this book, to help the customer look at his or her situation differently. It's earned by establishing credibility, demonstrating empathy, and proving that you are trustworthy. It is earned by doing your pre-call research, finding out as much as you can about the company and what problems it is facing. It is earned by asking questions in a nonthreatening way to confirm what you have already investigated and to find new needs and opportunities expressed by the customer.

"Hold on while we go over the SPIN Selling results."

Becoming a true consultant, partner, or trusted advisor requires careful listening. It requires you to make connections between what the customer needs and the benefits of your product or service. It implies the ability to allow the customer to talk at will about what he or she wants, anticipates, expects, hopes for, and worries about.

When all these behaviors are practiced, then you can make the critical jump to transform yourself into a consultative salesperson. Reading this book is a first step. It will require many more. It will also require patience, the willingness to learn, and some good coaching by a well trained mentor. More important, it will require your conviction that doing so will result in a better relationship with the customer and, ultimately, a win-win situation for both of you.

Only those who risk going too far can possibly find out how far one can go.
—T.S. Eliot

It Also Takes Action

Remember, anything worth doing, like asking questions, is worth doing wrong . . . until you get it right. Asking good questions, in the right order,

takes practice. And practice takes
action. Which reminds me of a
very old story about three little
frogs that were floating down the river on top of a leaf.
Suddenly, one of the frogs decides to jump into the river. How many
frogs are left on the leaf? I ask this question in my seminars and 90%
of the participants say that two frogs are left on the leaf. But there
are *three* frogs left on the leaf. Why three? Deciding to jump and
jumping are two different things altogether.

Happy jumping!

BURST INTO ACTION

*"Ideas are a dime a dozen, but the person who puts them into
practice is priceless."*

—Norman Vincent Peale

(1) Make sure that you don't act like an "expert" on your customers'
problems. Experts have a tendency to just tell their customers
what they need. Instead, approach your customers with a
beginner's perspective and listen—even though you are an
expert.

(2) Write down key Situation questions whose answers will provide
you with knowledge about prospects' situations—knowledge
you need in order to identify problems affecting the account.

(3) Make a list of the major problems your prospects might face.
Write down some good Problem questions.

(4) Write down Implication questions that deepen or accentuate the
importance of each major problem for your prospects.

(5) Document the connection of each of your offerings to each key
problem your customers have.

(6) When your customer is ready to buy, summarize the benefits of
your product or service that were accepted by the customer and
ask for some type of action to move the relationship or sale
forward.

TEST YOUR VALUE-SELLING SKILLS

Jerry L. Fritz

Jerry L. Fritz
is director of sales and customer service management
programs for Management
Institute, School of Business, University of Wisconsin-Madison. He directs,
coordinates, and instructs sales, sales management, and customer service
workshops and conferences for business professionals. His clients include
Monsanto, Trane Company, Arthur Andersen, and Blue Cross–Blue Shield.

Mr. Fritz was named 1996's marketing educator of the year by Sales and
Marketing Executives International. He is a featured speaker at *Inc.* magazine's
Semiannual Customer Service Strategies, Advanced Customer Service, and
Growing the Company Conferences. He has also spoken at annual meetings for
the International Customer Service Association and for Sales and Marketing
Executives International.

He knows how to address the training needs of industry practitioners
because he's faced the same type of business constraints they face. Before
joining Management Institute, Mr. Fritz spent more than 20 years in customer
contact and sales management roles for Roto-Rooter Services Company,
Catenation, and North American Van Lines, Inc.

Jerry L. Fritz, Management Institute, University of Wisconsin, 975 University Avenue,
Madison, WI 53706-1323; phone (800) 292-8964; fax (608) 262-4617; e-mail
JLF@mi.bus.wisc.edu.

TEST YOUR VALUE-SELLING SKILLS

Jerry L. Fritz

"Value is a relation between persons."
—Fernando Galiani, 1581

Research shows that, in today's competitive marketplace, 93% of customers seek *value* when they buy. The value your prospects and customers perceive in what you offer is not based solely on the relationship you establish with them—but it is in large part.

Consider this chapter a training session—one in which you will be coached on how to gain those skills which will help you differentiate yourself from the competition. In this training session, you will have the opportunity to complete exercises which will help you adapt ideas and philosophies and customize them to your circumstance and workplace. As a result of participating in this training, you will be able to differentiate yourself and gain a competitive advantage that will earn for you higher profits, greater market share, a stronger impact in your marketplace, and better relationships with your customers.

YOUR CUSTOMER'S PERCEPTION OF VALUE

Customers define value based on their unique set of criteria. They look at the value provided from you, their supplier, in a variety of ways. The five components of value are:

1 **Quality.** How are you improving your product or service? Customers want you to be continually improving your core offering to them. Quality is the first and most important component of value. An appropriate level of quality earns you the right to play in your marketplace.

> Quality in a service or product is not what you put into it. It is what the client or customer gets out of it.
>
> —Peter Drucker

Quality is not just how well your product or service works. The most subtle but impactful criteria that define quality are called "moments of truth." A moment of truth, as defined by Jan Carlzon of SAS, is any interaction that the customer has with your business. For example, a moment of truth occurs when an airline passenger pulls down her seat-back tray to find a coffee stain and infers that the airline is sloppy about engine maintenance!

Do your customers experience a positive impression when they interact with your business? If you want to offer value to your customers, you must be aware of the fact that *every* contact your customer has with your company is a moment of truth. And, that moment must be positive.

2 **Service support.** This includes far more than just customer service. It is all of those business components and de-

Customer Service Inside the Organization

One of the dangers is that people think of customer service as somebody else's job. We say to ourselves, "my job is sales" or "my job is data processing." But each of our jobs is broader than that—it's creating relationships and partnerships.

—Kristin Anderson, coauthor of *Delivering Knock Your Socks Off Service*

partments that support the sales promise to ensure that the customer receives exactly what the company committed to—if not more. Service support includes: defined customer satisfaction levels, order cycle, team commitment to customer expectations, an empowered contact team, a systematic recovery process, and warranties.

Service support is the extension of your commitment to the customer beyond the quality of your core product offering. Does your entire organization work together as a team? What lines of communication have you established in your organization? Each and every person in each and every department of your company must understand and contribute to the value the customer buys.

In many companies, product or brand managers coordinate all marketing for a product. In tomorrow's companies, product managers will also be the voice of the customer for their products. They will look for opportunities to thrill customers, such as after a problem has occurred (service recovery).

Service support also includes warranties. If a high-quality product has a warranty, which you earnestly stand behind, then trust and value are added to the sale of that product.

3 Customer relationships. Customers make it very clear that they like doing business with organizations that employ professional and likable salespeople, order entry staff, customer service representatives, delivery personnel, and others who have direct customer contact. The employees in your organization play a critical role in

Guarantees for Real-Time Info

Guaranteed for Life

Kaiser Permanente (an HMO) has been testing a program to offer on-the-spot refunds of copayment fees for any patient who is dissatisfied. Kaiser faced a lot of internal resistance to implementing the program, but very few clients ask for their money back. Key physician Robert Schultz said, "This is real-time feedback."

—Rick Crandall, *1001 Ways to Market Your Services: Even If You Hate to Sell*

how the customer interprets your value. How can you and your employees challenge yourselves to improve as customer contact professionals?

4 Delivery. What are the ingredients which make up delivery? To satisfy or exceed the customer's expectations regarding delivery, your organization must focus on the eight "rights" of delivery. These include, as defined or determined by your customer: right time, right price, right source/destination, right condition, right quantity, right mode, right product, and right packaging. How can you improve upon these rights? Your answer to that question and the action you then take will help you to differentiate yourself from the competition.

5 Investment. Is the cost of your products and services competitive within the marketplace? Do your customers believe that they are getting a return on their investment when they do business with you? It must be clear to the customer that the investment he or she makes regarding your quality, service support, delivery, and customer contact creates an appropriate package that is a good value.

HOW WELL DO YOU SELL VALUE?

To begin the training necessary to learn how to sell to your customer's perception of value, you must first challenge your current sales skills. Are you a top sales achiever? On the next two pages, you will find your first Training Session. As you complete this session, be completely honest. No one else will see your answers. Use the information from this exercise to analyze your sales skills.

Another Look

After you've completed the training session, look through your responses. Although all of the

Cost ≠ Price
Value means a good price for the quality you offer. You don't have to be the least expensive to be the most cost effective.

Training Exercise:
Are You a Top Sales Achiever?

What does it take to become a top achiever in sales? Answer the following questions to find out how you stack up.

	YES	NO	SOMETIMES
1. Do you listen to clients and prospects more than you talk to them?	☐	☐	☐
2. Do you emphasize what your product can do for the client rather than product features?	☐	☐	☐
3. Do you tailor your sales approach according to the prospect's individual situation?	☐	☐	☐
4. Do you carefully qualify prospects so that you see people with authority and strong sales potential?	☐	☐	☐
5. Do you look upon objections as an opportunity, not a threat?	☐	☐	☐
6. Do you anticipate objections and other hurdles and prepare appropriate answers?	☐	☐	☐
7. Do you probe for information by asking questions and then listening to the replies?	☐	☐	☐
8. Do you prospect and make qualifying calls so that if you lose a client, you won't jeopardize your sales goals?	☐	☐	☐
9. Do you always remember to ask for the commitment?	☐	☐	☐
10. Do you strive to improve your presentation?	☐	☐	☐
11. Do you always follow through with each customer, supplying requested information and answering questions?	☐	☐	☐
12. Do you know your product and the competition's well enough to differentiate between the two for the buyer?	☐	☐	☐

(continued)

	YES	NO	SOMETIMES
13. Do you employ time and territory management techniques to boost your efficiency?	☐	☐	☐
14. Do you set specific, written goals for yourself and refer to them often?	☐	☐	☐
15. Do you pat yourself on the back when you've done a good job—and maintain a positive outlook when things are tough?	☐	☐	☐
16. Do you focus on uncovering and then solving the customer's problems?	☐	☐	☐
17. Do you understand the different needs of each group influencing the purchase and how to meet them?	☐	☐	☐
18. Do you project enthusiasm for your product?	☐	☐	☐
19. Can you counter price objections by showing the superior value of your product?	☐	☐	☐
20. Do you increase sales by offering add-ons?	☐	☐	☐
21. Are you willing to go the extra mile to provide superior customer service?	☐	☐	☐

SCORING: Give yourself 3 points for every *Yes*, 2 points for every *Sometimes*, and 1 point for every *No*. Add the numbers to get your total score.

55-63	Congratulations! You're a superstar.
50-54	You're a successful professional salesperson.
40-49	Not bad, but with some focused effort, you could do better.
20-39	You need more training and coaching.

One-to-one customization helps you "achieve higher loyalty and value from [and for] those customers worth the most to your enterprise."

—Don Peppers and Martha Rogers,
Enterprise One to One

questions are important, some are critical to your success if you indeed want to practice the philosophy of value-added selling. Pay particularly close attention to the following questions:

QUESTION #2: **Do you understand the applications of your product?** Do you understand enough about your customers to apply your "solution" to their situation or problem?

QUESTION #7: **Do you probe for information by asking questions and then listening to the replies?** Have two to three probes ready for every major question you ask. Top-producing salespeople show their expertise not by what they tell the customer, but by what they ask the customer. It is through thorough questioning that you can clearly understand what the customer wants. In turn, you then provide the value that the customer truly needs through a one-to-one customization.

QUESTION #11: **Do you always follow through with each customer, supplying requested information and answering questions?** A salesperson's job is not to sell, but rather to educate and understand, and then offer value when it is appropriate. Good salespeople are consultants (and more—as described in Chapter 2). They are experts regarding their industries. They ask skillful questions and probe for additional information. When they know what the customer needs, they ask themselves: "Can we meet or exceed the expectations that the customer has described?"

QUESTION #16: **Focus on getting inside the customer's head so that you can understand exactly what he or she is**

Off-the-Shelf Solutions Won't Do

The better a salesperson is at creatively marshaling all available resources to address a customer's strategic needs, the stronger the customer relationship becomes.

The ability to solve problems creatively is one of the characteristics of top salespeople. As a vice president of Scott Paper said, "Selling will be a balance of standardization and customization. We'll be able to customize a unique solution to meet each customer's needs. This is the essence of consultative selling."

—Learning International, Inc.

facing. One of the problems salespeople face is overcoming their desire to talk about their products and services the minute they get in front of a customer who is willing to listen. That is the last thing you want to do.

The first goal in any customer relationship is to build trust and rapport. The second step is to understand the customer's needs. The third part of the process, if appropriate, is to show how your organization can satisfy those needs.

QUESTION #17: **You have more than one person in a business making decisions today.** Due to restructuring, reengineering, and flattening, you have a situation when you will seldom have one manager or one person making major decisions. Often the bigger the investment, the more people or departments are involved in the decision. The value-added sales representative today must get inside the organization and determine who the buying influencers are and identify their "stake" in the purchase.

QUESTION #18: **Do you project enthusiasm for your product or service?** If not, then find another product to sell! When it comes time for the actual commitment, the customer will look you in the eye. If you do not truly believe, well, let's just say it will probably be time to resume prospecting.

QUESTION #20: **Make sure that anything that you add on to the product increases the**

Raving Fans Sell for You

Sheldon Bowles is an entrepreneur from Canada, who, in the 1970s when everyone was going to self-service gas stations, decided it was the perfect time to go to full service. He created a series of gas stations across Western Canada called Domo Gas.

Sheldon's vision of perfection was that going to one of his stations would be like an Indianapolis 500 pit stop. All the attendants were dressed in red jumpsuits. When you drove in, they would race to your car. One would begin working under your hood, one would pump gas, while yet another person would ask you to step out of the car, offer you a cup of coffee and a newspaper, and "dustbust" your car.

Sheldon's stations blew away the competition. They created raving fans. That's where the concept came from. Raving fans are customers who are so excited about what you do that they become part of your sales force.

—Ken Blanchard

value, as interpreted by the customer. Don't add things to a product or service just because they are available. You do not *sell* customers anything. You provide what they *need* in their situation to help them.

QUESTION #21: **Make sure customers truly want and need the service you provide, and that it is offered to them in such a way that they see its value.** And you have to make sure that your service is legendary!

How did you do on these eight questions? Plan how you can move each of your "no" and "sometimes" answers to "yes"! The more yes answers you can achieve, the more you'll turn your customers into raving fans who become an unpaid sales force for you.

WHAT ARE YOU SELLING?

What do you actually sell to the customer? If you describe your product or service in answer to this question, then there is a problem. It is not what the customer is buying. The customer wants the true benefit that the product provides. It's the old story of the man who entered the hardware store. He did not come seeking a drill with a $3/8''$ bit—he just wanted a $3/8''$ hole!

Position your product or service in a way that it is not feature- or product-oriented. Most products in the same class look pretty much the same. If there is no additional benefit or value that you are able to describe from the customer's point of view, the only decision the customer will have to make is "who is cheapest"? And, that's a game you don't want to play.

Positioning

Positioning is a concept developed by Jack Trout and Al Ries. It is how people perceive your product or service in relation to similar products.

THE BUYER-SALESPERSON INTERACTION PROCESS

Buying is a process, not an event. Most sales today, in business-to-business selling, are not a one-call close. Most sales occur over several weeks, several months, and in some cases years, for large capital investments. Nevertheless, you usually are looking at several sales calls on a business-to-business opportunity before there is enough information shared both ways so that you can determine that there is a

> ### It Takes Time to Build Relationships
> The average sale takes about six contacts to make. The average salesperson quits after two. For many services like law, the average sale takes 12 contacts.

fit—count on it taking multiple calls to gain a commitment. One thing you must to do if you want to be trained to be a good value-added seller is to persevere and work to build the relationship with your customers.

Reaching a Buying Decision

There are four psychological stages that customers go through to make buying decisions. Correspondingly, there are sales skills which are required of the salesperson to get the customer through those stages.

In which of the areas (listed in the box on the next page) do you need further training? I'll cover Stages 1 and 4 here. Other chapters cover Stage 1 further on relationship building, Stage 2 on Needs Analysis, and Stage 3 on Presentations.

Stage 1: Initial impressions. This is the stage where you initiate contact with a potential customer. This is also when you need to begin to establish trust. If you do a good job of establishing rapport, that will account for 45% of whether or not you will be successful with that customer. This is the most important stage in the selling process. If you can show the customer that he or she can

Buying Decisions: Matching Buyer's Stage with Salesperson's Skills

BUYER'S STAGE	SALESPERSON'S SKILLS
1. Initial impressions	1. Personal preparation; interpersonal skills 2. Customer's perception of your differentiated approach
2. Problem and implication analysis	3. Questioning 4. Listening & note-taking 5. Summarizing
3. Consultative positioning	6. Presenting customer-focused solutions 7. Customer-focused proposals
4. Confirmation	8. Resolving concerns—overcoming/preventing objections 9. Gain-gain negotiating 10. Gaining commitment 11. Techniques for reassurance and follow-through

trust you, the rest of your job will be easier and the odds tilt in your favor to gain a new customer.

The salesperson's skills required of you to make those positive initial impressions include the following:

Personal preparation. Are you prepared to do the job? Do you know how to relate to and with the customer? Being prepared means being knowledgeable about your product or service and its application to the customer's needs and situation. If you do not feel prepared, take the time to learn how your product is put together or how your service is developed in your organization. Use that knowledge and experience to gain credibility and trust.

Customer's perception of your differentiated approach. Once you are familiar with your products and services, can you present a differentiated approach that shows how you are better than, or different from, your competition? Your approach alone can help you gain a competitive advantage and enable you to gain tremendous trust.

Your approach in the initial impressions stage should include these three steps:

Step 1. State your call objective or purpose.

Position yourself as a problem solver. Begin by:

- making your opening clarification statement, then
- transitioning into the question-asking/Customer Needs Analysis process.

The opening clarification statement should identify the way(s) in which your company can help the customer. These include helping the prospect to:

- gain a competitive advantage
- reduce operating costs
- increase margin/profit levels
- enhance the level of quality
- improve productivity
- increase their ROI through products and services you provide
- increase efficiency

Ask appropriate questions. Begin your initial contact with the customer by saying something like the following, "In order for us to determine if we can help you in this/these way(s), may I ask you a few questions?"

Your questions should help the contact identify and focus in on one or more of the seven areas

---

Improve Sales by Improving Knowledge

Want your people to sell more products? Make sure they know as much as possible. A Nordstrom buyer in San Francisco has monthly meetings with all salespeople to discuss new merchandise. She also invites vendors to the meetings so they can comment on key selling points of their products. "If I just buy a line, it may sell okay, but if I teach the salespeople about the quality and value of the product, and how to present it, it may sell wonderfully," she says.

—*Executive Edge* newsletter

listed above. You also need to uncover basic information about the company—what its problem area(s) might be, what the implications to this person and the company might be if the problem is or is not resolved, and what the ultimate objectives, mission, and vision are. You also need to find out the contact's vision of the solution.

Step 2. Identify what other departments and respective managers and officers are affected by not preventing or solving the identified problem. Take time to clearly understand the total impact throughout their organization.

Step 3. Help the customer identify how his or her customers, both internal and external, are affected by this situation. How can you impact the customer's customers?

From *Key Account Selling* by Mack Hanan

STAGE 2. Problem and implication analysis. This stage is also referred to as CNA (Customer Needs Analysis). This particular stage accounts for 30% of whether or not you will be successful. Once you have made a positive first impression, established and maintained trust, and worked the customer through an appropriate Customer Needs Analysis process, you are 75% of the way home to building and maintaining a long-lasting relationship with your customer. (See the Chapters on Needs Analysis and Listening for more details.)

STAGE 3. Consultative positioning. This stage accounts for 15% of whether or not you will be successful with your customers. A consultative sales approach is more effective than a traditional product-centered (features/advantages/

benefits) sales approach in today's competitive marketplace.

The consultative approach is about learning how you can make a contribution to your customer's bottom-line productivity and profitability. This is a systematic approach to prevent or resolve problems. It goes beyond product requirements to a more comprehensive view of the prospect's business problems. You need to determine how the problem or service can not only solve or prevent the problem, but also how you can be an active part of the solution. (See Chapters 1 and 2 for more details on how to reach the level of trusted consultant—or even higher.)

STAGE 4. Confirmation. This stage is also called customer retention. It accounts for 10% of your sales success but as much as 90% of your companies profits! American Airlines did some quick calculations and found that if they'd had one more or less customer on each flight in a given year, the difference in revenues would have been about $114 million.

If you have come this far, this is merely a "Don't blow it!" stage. At this stage, you must identify those behaviors you will need to practice in order to grow the positive relationship with your customer (see box).

Relationship Builders

Following is a list of ideas for you to maintain reassurance and follow-through with your customers:

- Make frequent contacts (phone, mail, fax, e-mail) with your customers.
- Provide a continual account review process.
- Be honest at all times.
- Offer alternative choices, recommendations and ideas (including others' products or services when they are appropriate).
- Maintain personal presence in front of the customer.
- Measure the level of satisfaction.
- Maintain communication regarding the project's status.
- Remain customer attentive after the commitment is made.

And then go the "Extra Mile." These are additional ways you and your company can be seen as offering additional value to your customers.

- Reinforce the buying decision immediately (follow up notes, compliments).
- Make sure the customer gets what you promised.
- Make a non-selling follow-up call.
- Keep good records and stay in touch.
- Turn your customers into raving fans.

DEVELOPING YOUR ACTION PLAN

Are you prepared to sell to your customer's perception of value? From this "training" program, what have you identified as your areas of opportunity? What would you like to work on to pump up your sales? Continued training is not an event but a well planned process intent on providing lifelong learning.

The first step to improved results begins with the initiation of an action plan. Use a worksheet like the one in the box below. Also see the suggestions at the end of each chapter, and the last chapter in particular for setting up an implementation system.

For best results, share this plan with your supervisor or a helpful other to plan for their support, follow-up meetings, and discussions of results.

CONCLUSION: STAYING FIT

You have completed your training session to improve the level of value you and your company offer your customers. But as in any "fitness"

Your Action Plan for Self-Improvement

List the three behaviors you would like to improve	How will you monitor your progress (must be observable and measurable)	Goal (specific, quantifiable, measurable)	Goal will be achieved by (date)
1._____	1. _____	1. _____	1. _____
2._____	2. _____	2. _____	2. _____
3._____	3. _____	3. _____	3. _____

program, you must commit to practice what you have learned. Take the time to put your intentions into practice. Communicate your standards and goals with your internal and external customers.

Record your experiences, successes, and failures. Refer back to the Training Exercise in this chapter, regularly, to monitor your progress and keep in touch. And most of all, have fun! Selling is a challenge, an ongoing test of your knowledge and skills that can offer a lifetime of personal and career success.

BURST INTO ACTION

"Successful people get ahead during the time other people waste."

—Henry Ford

(1) List the extra value you offer when people buy from you, such as special service, consulting, networking for them, and so forth.

(2) List specific ways you and your assistants can build personal relationships with customers.

(3) Create a worksheet showing the difference between price and cost over time for each product and service you offer. Help customers define value.

(4) List all the ways your products and services are used by customers. Can you share unusual uses with other customers?

(5) Create a chart of the different kinds of customers you have, their needs, and their perceptions of value.

(6) Survey your customers. Ask them what new things would help them in a world where cost were no object.

(7) Study how you can help your customers serve their customers better.

NETWORKING FOR SALES

Renee P. Walkup

Renee P. Walkup, president and founder of SalesPEAK, Inc.®, is an expert in sales, marketing, trade shows, and professional communication. Skills acquired from 17 years of corporate experience allow her to assist clients in building their businesses through the implementation of methods that have proven successful time and time again.

Thousands have made positive changes in their professional and personal lives after attending Ms. Walkup's programs. Some of her clients include The Coca-Cola Company, Turner Broadcasting, International Thompson Publishing, Hewlett Packard, and Outward Bound.

Ms. Walkup has been a guest on various radio and television programs, and is a contributing writer to several business publications, including *The Atlanta Business Chronicle*. She is listed in the *International Who's Who of Entrepreneurs*.

An active member of the business community, Ms. Walkup is involved in Business and Technology Alliance (BETA), Women's ORT, Board of Directors Network, Georgia Speakers Association, and National Association of Women Business Owners (NAWBO).

Renee P. Walkup, SalesPEAK, Inc.®, 1896 Winchester Trail, Atlanta, GA 30341; phone (770) 220-0832; fax (770) 220-0833; e-mail walkupto@aol.com; www.salespeak@mindspring.com.

NETWORKING FOR SALES

Renee P. Walkup

"Others things being equal, people do business with people they like. Others things not being equal, people still do business with people they like."

—Mark McCormack, *What They Don't Teach You at Harvard Business School*

Personal networking is your best way to get new customers and keep existing ones.

Think of networking like a web of hyperlinks online. Somewhere you make an acquaintance. You hit it off by uncovering in conversation that you attended the same college, grew up in the same neighborhood, or prepare spaghetti sauce using the same secret ingredient. You like each other. There's a common bond that connects the two of you. Your relationship-building skills help it become permanent.

Eventually you begin to talk about your work. Your new friend provides you with a potential customer's phone number and a comment, "Use my name." After contacting this referral, you're provided with another potential buyer. You secure a sale. One link leads to another. The web is growing. And guess what? So is your business!

NETWORKING THROUGH GROUPS

For networking through groups, you'll want to target those organizations where you're likely to have genuine common links. There are four categories of organizations that you should consider joining. First is leisure groups where you'll enjoy the activities even if you don't meet anyone— but you will. You'll share a common interest with other attendees.

Next, think about your business interests. Join an organization that your targeted customers attend. Then look for groups with complementary businesses with whom you can partner in order to grow your sales. Finally, join an organization with those who are in a similar business as yours so that you can establish a reputation with your "own" and also receive leads from these like-minded individuals.

> ### Networking Math
>
>
>
> A Stanford study by Joel Podolny and James Baron showed that small increases in the size of your network can double your odds of success. If your existing network is not producing much in the way of referrals, try to add 10% more high-quality contacts. That 10% can double your results.
>
> —Rick Crandall, *1001 Ways to Market Your Services: Even If You Hate to Sell*

Here are some examples of these four types of groups. Let's say you are a technical writer who wants to build your business. Most of your clients are medium-sized software companies in your metropolitan area. Your favorite pastime is tennis. Here's what your networking organizations might look like:

- a tennis club near the technology park
- a local business and technology organization

- the local American Marketing Association
- a metropolitan technical writers guild

A 10-TIP PLAN FOR NETWORKING

Now that you've joined organizations like the ones listed above, how do you know what to do once you get there? Or better yet, *before* you arrive! Based on years of experience and face-to-face research, I recommend the following 10 tips that will build your network and grow your business.

Tip 1: Plan Ahead

Before you arrive at any function, decide on your goals and your message.

If you want to expand your database, then you'll want to meet as many people as you can and gather their business cards. However, if you are a member of the organization, you can probably get a membership directory and enter those names into your database much more efficiently.

Perhaps your objective is to reconnect with someone you met either at this organization or somewhere else. Contact her in advance and ask if she is attending the function. Indicate that you are looking forward to seeing her. Do not, under any circumstances, imply that you are going to attempt to sell her something, or generally pester her. Remember, your networking objective is to build rapport so that you can eventually do business with her or her contacts.

Another objective may include meeting a specific person who you know will be there. In this case, scan the room for him when you arrive. See if he's talking with an acquaintance of yours or if he is standing alone. Don't be shy, go ahead and

Mingling is like going fishing. You cast out your line, and if they aren't biting, you move to another spot. Develop a "line" of small talk that puts other people at their ease and then find people who enjoy it.
—Don Gabor,
Fifty Ways to Improve Your Conversations

introduce yourself using one of the conversation openers included in Tip 4.

As part of your plan, project your message by dressing appropriately. How do you want others to perceive you? If you want to look authoritative, wear a dark suit. Black, navy, and charcoal gray are dominant power colors. Want to stand out? Wear bright red, deep purple, or a bright shade of yellow in your clothing. Teal is the "friendly color." A splash of teal in a tie, scarf, blouse, or pocket square is inviting to strangers.

Tip 2: Read the Room

When most of us walk into a roomful of strangers, those pesky stomach butterflies begin to form. These hints and tips on reading the room should assist you in getting those butterflies to fly in formation!

When you arrive at the function, take a moment to survey the room. Who do you want to meet? Is the person you want to reconnect with there? Again, keeping your goal in mind, plan your first approach.

If you want to meet new people, look for someone who is like you—we usually connect best with those individuals most like

Networking "Rooms"

us. For example, I am an extrovert who likes to wear bright clothes, talk with my hands, and engage people in conversation. So when I arrive at a get-together, I look for a person who looks friendly, outgoing, and confident. That's where *I* begin because those are the individuals with whom I feel most comfortable. With what types of people do you feel most at ease?

The main point to remember here is that you want to get those butterflies flying in formation *while* you go about accomplishing your networking goals. The sooner you feel comfortable in your surroundings, the faster you'll begin developing relationships that will lead to more business.

Tip 3: Set Yourself Apart with Better Introductions

It's one of those often-overlooked skills: introducing yourself professionally and knowing how to properly introduce others. To introduce yourself, there are four steps:

(1) Make good eye contact.

(2) Connect with a firm handshake.

(3) Smile as you clearly say your name.

(4) Repeat the person's name ("Good to meet you, Joanne.").

When introducing yourself, give a little more than just your name and business. Add something personal or subtly mention the benefits your customers receive—but take care not to sound pushy or overbearing.

Also practice the fine art of introducing others. Incorporate this skill into your repertoire and you'll find yourself making friends and business contacts that can last a lifetime!

One way you can immediately demonstrate that you're a networker who helps others is to make introductions. Pick people who can help each other. You can even introduce people you don't know by acting as a "host" at the meeting to help people mingle.

Remember Names Better

When meeting a person for the first time, make a mental note of the name by associating the name with something familiar. For example, Joy Redfern has auburn hair. Also, repeat the name several times during the first few minutes of your conversation to lock the name into your memory.

Conversely, when you're introducing yourself, give the person a hook on which to hang your name: for example, "Hello, my name is Maggie Holmes—no relation to Sherlock, although I do try to uncover value for my clients."

HELLO, MY NAME IS

Maggie Holmes

When introducing people at a function. Use this format:

- Introduce a younger person to an older person.
- Introduce a peer in your company to a peer in another company.
- Introduce a fellow executive to a customer or client.

As a professional networker, you can successfully acquaint people with each other by offering a sentence or two of information to the people you are introducing. This introduction may go somewhat like this:

"Margo, I'd like you to meet John Miller with Atlantic Coast Supply. John was just promoted to National Sales Manager."

"John, this is Margo Adams. Margo is an incredibly talented speaker. She recently shared the platform with Norman Schwartzkopf."

After this type of introduction, you have served your networking contacts well because they both now have several points of departure from which they can begin a conversation.

Not only that, but you have just elevated yourself as a valuable contact and a professional. Both John and Margo will respect you more for linking them into a potentially valuable connection. Guess where they will go when they can use your products and services? Not only that, both of them will be more inclined to recommend you to their circles of influence.

Tip 4: How to Open a Conversation and Keep It Going

Small talk is a big deal when it comes to networking simply because we all need a place to start. Since geographic, cultural, and other vari-

---

The Business Card

You can always tell an amateur networker because he will foist a business card on you immediately after the introduction. This is the equivalent of being hounded at the supermarket to sample the cheese at the deli counter. The best time to exchange cards is after some rapport has been established.

Don't have your home phone number printed on your card. Instead, hand write it when giving a new customer or contact your card. This simple act makes the recipient feel special.

The word, even the most contradictory word, preserves contact—it is silence which isolates.

—Thomas Mann

ables may come into play when beginning a conversation, the safest and easiest place to begin is with *what you know.*

Your small talk may begin something like this:

"How long have you been a member of this organization?"

"What did you think of the last luncheon we had at this hotel?"

"Were you a member of this group when..."

"When was the last time you attended a function with this group?"

"So, what did you think of the speaker's talk this morning?"

Prepare for spontaneous conversation. Before you leave for a networking event, take a few minutes and write down five or six opening questions to get someone talking.

The idea here is to get the person talking so that you are *listening* and *learning.* Take the first question, for example. Let's say your new friend responds with: "I've been a member for about six years. In fact, I was president in '95 and have stayed very active since."

For you, a new member or a visitor of this group, this person has just provided very valuable information. Now is your opportunity to discover more about the group. If you are at the function to meet particular people, this person will probably know them. And since she is a past president, she is most probably in a position to have networked with many people. All this information from just one question!

A logical follow-up question may sound like this: "In the six years you've been involved in the

---

Small Talk Tips

- Make sure your first questions are open-ended to get the person to talk.
- Keep the questions positive or neutral. Avoid negativity.
- The weather is usually a boring subject. Show more creativity.
- Avoid beginning the conversation with anything too personal.

organization, what major changes and initiatives have taken place?"

Now you've got your new friend talking and you can sit back and pay close attention by practicing valuable listening skills. (See also Chapter 8 on listening.)

While you're listening, rapport is being built. She's probably thinking that you're interested, friendly, and confident. And keep in mind, you've hardly said a word! What you *have* done is indicated genuine interest and an ability to listen well—traits difficult to come by in many business situations.

A useful rule of thumb is to talk no more than 40% of the time and to listen 60%. This formula assures a two-way conversation, without your dominating the conversation. Sometimes you'll be considered the best conversationalist when you only talk 25% of the time—just enough to ask questions to keep the other person going.

Other Conversation Ideas

- community activities
- hobbies
- the arts
- vacations
- schools
- hometowns and neighborhoods
- favorite cartoon strips
- sports
- famous people
- current events
- places lived
- travel
- exercise
- first jobs
- food and restaurants
- TV shows
- shopping
- children

Areas to Avoid

- politics
- personal health problems
- prejudices
- off-color jokes
- religion
- questions that are too personal
- gossip
- insincere compliments
- a hard sell of any kind

Tip 5: Do Something for Them

If you want people to scratch your back, get *your* back scratcher out. Today, with everyone too busy to even return phone calls to friends, how can we expect virtual strangers to go the extra mile to assist us in building our customer bases? The answer is simple—if you're ready to contribute to helping your new friends' businesses grow.

If you meet a new contact and she's telling you about her business, immediately begin thinking about who you might know she can network with.

You may even ask her, "What's a good lead for you?" Perhaps it's a potential customer, an investor, a vendor, a strategic partner, or even another professional networker who has numerous contacts and abilities to connect people. Now that you have some of these people in mind, don't be shy. Communicate about who you know and why she may find it beneficial to contact them. Invite her to use your name when she calls.

If the contact is particularly important, you may want to offer to call the individual first by way of an introduction. This type of entree is significant in today's business environment.

Let's assume you have provided the information to your new friend as mentioned. Even if the person is unsuccessful in securing a beneficial business relationship with your contact, she will almost always reciprocate with a lead or leads for you. Isn't this what this back scratching thing is all about?

Tip 6: Practice Active Listening Skills

We all know about not interrupting and not thinking about the next question when others are talking. However, are you truly aware of what your body language might be saying while you are listening?

For example, many people nod frequently in seeming agreement. This nodding can make you appear overly eager or insincere. If you are a "nodder," be aware of this habit and concentrate on nodding only when it's appropriate in the conversation.

Often, at networking functions, a person will scan the room while engaged in a conversation. This is exceedingly rude and sug-

---

Eye Contact

When you talk to others, eye contact achieves the right connection. About five seconds of steady eye contact is appropriate. Less than that suggests that you're nervous or don't want to make connections. Much more than that can be seen as intimacy or intimidation. Five seconds is also about how long it takes to complete a thought or a sentence.

—Bert Decker, *You've Got to Be Believed to Be Heard*

gests that the person with whom you are talking is not good enough to share your time. So be aware of your eyes and make sure they are focused on your new acquaintance.

Another significant listening skill is to smile and audibly send messages that you are interested in the discourse and enjoying the conversation.

Pay close attention to important key words or phrases from your new contact. These assertions may provide you with clues to assist you in scratching his back by uncovering real needs that he has. Or you may find a way for him to scratch yours.

For example, someone may say, "It seems to me that if I just had a system in my office, I could get more work done in less time." Perhaps you network with a professional organizer and can share a phone number with your new contact.

Maybe one of your networking friends is an independent executive assistant who can work with this person. How about recommending a software product that helped organize your office or a particular filing system that you implemented? Another suggestion is to recommend a time management course that you've taken. Now you're becoming an even more valuable resource to those who know you because you are there to assist by thinking out of the box and offering solutions.

> ## How to Get New Contacts to Talk More
>
> Use open-ended questions as described in Tip 4. Use the five Ws and an H along with a T. Ask:
> - who
> - what
> - where
> - when
> - why
> - how
> - tell (Tell me about...)
>
> That will keep them talking and you listening and learning!

Tip 7: Follow Up with a Personal Note

In these days of word processing, I am always delighted to find how impressed people are when I take the time to write a handwritten note. It sends the positive message that you care. And how much

Big Effects from a Few Words

A fellow who attended a speech I once gave to several hundred folks dropped me a line: "Nice job! Thought you might enjoy the attached." The attached was a clipping from his local paper about a company that had speeded up delivery of its products—a topic I'd gotten worked up about during my speech.

You know what—I've reread his scribble a couple of times, and I'll probably put it in my save box. "Nice job!" No big deal? Well, it is to me.

We wildly underestimate the power of the tiniest personal touch. And of all personal touches, I find the short, handwritten "nice job" note to have the highest impact.

WHICH CAME FIRST— THANK YOUs OR SUCCESS?

I think there's a strong correlation between the little thank you notes I get and the busyness, fortune, and fame of those who send them. That is, the more busy, rich, and famous they are, the more likely I am to get a note.

One pen pal scrawls brief handwritten responses on the backs of letters I send him. I love it, and have copied his habit.

Again: A tiny human touch goes a long way.

—Tom Peters

time does it really take to write out a message?

Many people tell me that they are so out of practice at writing that their penmanship is unacceptably illegible. It doesn't matter. Just as we were taught from childhood, "It's the thought that counts," and it *does*! Setting yourself apart from the word-processing population is a real plus in building relationships in today's business world.

You may write this note on a business note card, a postcard, a standard "Thank You" card, or on any type of greeting card that reflects your personality and message. You can even have custom ones printed.

Another key relationship-building hint is to include a significant bit of information in the note. It should be slightly personal but not overly so because, remember, this note is probably ending up at the person's office.

Here's an example. If your new friend mentions an upcoming vacation, you may want to wish her a relaxing, enjoyable trip. That's fine. However, if she revealed a story about an unpleasant surgery that she recently experienced, leave that out. It's too personal. The bottom line is, send the note and personalize it appropriately.

Tip 8: Use a Database

It doesn't take long to realize that keeping up with business cards on a Rolodex is terribly inefficient, tedious, and time-wasting. Then there's the question of how to file them—alphabetically by last name or company name, by type of business—there are so many choices and none of them satisfy every need every time.

To manage your contacts more efficiently, you *must* have a database which includes names, companies, phone numbers, e-mail addresses, types of business, referral contacts, and more. If done correctly, you can find anyone, anytime, and with a minimum of effort.

By keeping these records up to date, anytime you or one of your networking contacts needs a service, you can look up the information with a touch of a few keys. This is ten times more efficient than flipping through a Rolodex for a card that someone gave you six months ago.

Do It Soon

If cards are worth collecting, they're worth recording. After each networking function, enter your new contacts' information into your database. Otherwise you'll end up with a pile of cards and not remember anything about the people. Key in where you met them, vital statistics, their industry and job function, and any other information you learned (where a spouse works, hobbies, and so forth).

TIP 9: Keep in Touch

You think you've worked hard up to this point—attending functions, meeting virtual strangers, listening well, building relationships, exchanging cards, following up with notes, and the rest. Now the *challenging* part of your work begins! In order to network to grow your sales, you have to keep in touch with your new contacts. That's how lasting relationships are built.

There are several approaches that you can take. They are:

- honoring honors
- personalizing interests
- contacting by group
- using invitations
- attending more functions
- A-Z weekly contact system

Honor honors. Keep up with the news. You'll find contacts' names and accomplishments in the newspaper, in the local business journal, and in trade magazines. When you see someone you know featured, jot the contact a note, congratulating them on that recent award or honor. If appropriate, include the clipping. This makes your contact feel important and special that you have recognized her in the news.

Personalize interests. This contact takes place when you see or hear of a particular item of interest to someone you know. For example, you happen to know that your contact rides horses and is looking to buy one. You are on an airplane reading the airline magazine and notice an article on purchasing and boarding horses. Clip it out and send it with a note to your new friend. Mention that you saw the article and were thinking of him, so you thought he might enjoy it. Who doesn't want to feel special in this way?

Contact by group. Grouping your networking contacts in your database provides you with an efficient way of staying in touch with people who have something in common. For example, in my database, I have listed a group of women whom I like to invite to my networking parties. About every six weeks, I fax them an invitation to come to my house for food, drink and fun. Every one of them receives an invitation even though they can't all come every time.

Another way of contacting people by group is through your marketing efforts. For example, if you are targeting business with software firms, you may want to group them in your database and send a brochure or new product announcement to them. To add a more personalized punch, jot a note on the brochure. Each recipient will appreciate the special touch.

Use invitations. Do you want to develop the relationship with a networking contact? Invite her to attend a function with you. This is an excellent way to get to know your new contact better. She will spend some time with you and you can learn more about her business, building on the budding relationship. Who knows, you may even introduce each other to new contacts!

Attend more functions. If you want to get to know your contacts better, then attend more functions where your contacts meet. For example, if you've joined an organization, make sure you go to the meetings or breakfasts often so that you can stay in touch with your new friends because they'll be there, too!

Schedule your contacts. Try the A-Z weekly contact system. This method of staying in touch is designed especially for those of you who are systematic. Each week you will contact two letters of the alphabet via telephone, voice mail, e-mail, direct mail, or in person. This system allows you to stay in touch with your contacts quarterly, at

JANUARY

					1	2	3
4	5	6	7	8	9	10
Contact A-Bs						
11	12	13	14	15	16	17
Contact C-Ds						
18	19	20	21	22	23	24
Contact E-Fs						
25	26	27	28	29	30	31
Contact G-Hs						

least. So in January, week 1, you connect with people whose names begin with an A and B, and so forth. Each quarter, you will be contacting all 26 letters in the alphabet again, allowing you to stay in touch and reminding people that you are around and thriving.

Trade Introductions

When you're at a networking event with a friend, ask the friend which persons he or she knows. As the friend points out different people around the room, you can ask for an introduction to someone you don't know. A personal introduction smooths the way. Then introduce your friend to one of your contacts in return!

Tip 10: Never Give Up

You may find that you joined an organization or attended several functions that resulted in no business or contacts. That's OK. Sometimes a group that appears to be a perfect fit for your business ends up as a dud. The reasons may vary. Perhaps there are too many people in your business at the same function, and you are the new kid on the block. Maybe the group is social, and members prefer not to conduct business with each other. Another possibility is that you chose the group because of a friend's recommendation, but it doesn't turn out to be your target market after all.

Try another group. Attend several functions and apply the tools discussed here. I can assure you that if you implement the strategies outlined in this chapter, your circle of influence will grow and you will reap the benefits while you are helping others build their businesses.

Finally, keep in mind that developing and building relationships *takes time*. If networking were immediate, we'd all have more business than we could handle in no time at all! Forging these long-term business friendships means putting forth effort, with sincerity and integrity, and then staying in touch. Attend functions and you will soon see that networking will grow your sales!

BURST INTO ACTION

"Success usually depends on two methods only—energy and perseverance."

—Goethe

(1) List the personal activities—like hiking or bridge—that you've been meaning to do more of. Now schedule yourself to do them in the next month. Then pick one to do regularly where you can make new friends.

(2) Pick a business group to attend where you will meet potential customers. If you're not sure which ones, ask your current customers what groups they go to. Often they'll introduce you to others.

(3) Pick a group to attend where you'll meet people from businesses that you could partner with because they sell to your customers. (For instance, an accountant picks a bankers' group.)

(4) Pick a group to attend where you'll meet colleagues in your own industry.

(5) Write a 20-word introduction for yourself that includes more than your name and business. Try to include a benefit to customers or a memorable personal touch.

(6) If you don't like small talk, prepare five topics you'll be comfortable talking about with strangers.

(7) Decide how you'll keep in touch with contacts. A personal postcard? Phone calls? E-mail? Faxed cartoons?

(8) Set up a usable database and enter all new contacts regularly.

LEADING SALES PRODUCERS LISTEN

Greg Bauer

Greg Bauer
is an international professional speaker, consultant, trainer, and writer on proven communication and listening skills, ideas, and techniques. As a Guru of Listening, Mr. Bauer assists corporations, associations, and individuals in developing their customer service, sales, and management abilities by helping them benefit from discovering the attributes of the "Lost Art of Listening."

During his professional speaking career, he has received many honors including chapter Member of the Year Award from the Professional Speakers Association of Michigan and The National Speakers Association; Circle of Excellence Award from Carlson Learning Company International; Distinguished Toastmaster (the highest designation awarded by Toastmasters International); and a recognized business leader as a professional speaker and consultant by the Strathmore Registry International.

Among the many clients Mr. Bauer has assisted with their listening and communication skills are: American Electric Power, Hugh O'Brian International Youth Foundation, AT&T, Society for Women in Transportation, Hospitality Sales and Marketing Association International, Kraft General Goods, Microsoft, and Frito-Lay, Inc.

Greg Bauer, Greg Bauer & Associates, Inc., P.O. Box 931, Grandville, MI 49468-0931; phone (616) 669-4200; fax (616) 669-0601; e-mail GBA Listen@aol.com.

LEADING SALES PRODUCERS LISTEN

Greg Bauer

"It is the province of knowledge to speak and it is the privilege of wisdom to listen."

—Oliver Wendell Holmes

There's an old sales saying that you have two ears and one mouth and should use them in that proportion. Apparently, this thought on the wisdom of being a listener goes back more than 2000 years to at least the early Greeks. Witness these quotes:

"We have two ears and only one tongue in order that we may hear more and speak less." (Diogenes)

"Nature has given to men one tongue, but two ears, that we may hear from others twice as much as we speak." (Epictetus)

That's just about the ratio I recommend: Listening 70% and Speaking 30%.

By utilizing the attributes of effective listening, you will:

- increase sales
- increase profitability on both a personal and corporate level
- learn more about the world and people around you
- be seen as more intelligent and a better conversationalist
- be liked more for your company

Tom Peters says we need to become obsessed with listening. He notes that everyone gives lip service to listening, but that salespeople instead start trying to "educate" the prospect or customer about the benefits of buying what they're selling.

> ### Listening for Sales
>
> Along with sympathetic listening, the ability to understand and identify with the goals of the speaker helps in every phase of the sales process, according to Lucete Comer at Purdue University. Research showed that sales reps with higher listening skills were better in all phases of the sales process, such as approach and after-sales support.

THE S.A.L.E.S. FORMULA

When you become obsessed with listening, both you and the speaker benefit. Sales will be perceived as a respected helping profession only when listening is the first skill trained. One way to overview the skills involved in listening is the S.A.L.E.S. Formula.

PRACTICE MAKES THE DIFFERENCE

Accomplished pianists, professional speakers, and Olympic gold-medal winners are not born with their impressive abilities and talents. Nor are people born as effective listeners.

Listening is also an art form that needs to be continually practiced, modified, and refined. An

The S.A.L.E.S. Formula

S ecure the conversation each time you are exchanging ideas with a prospect by listening. Then listen again. Then listen some more. The one who is really listening is the one in control of the conversation (and the sale).

A ssess the situation by actively listening. Utilize open-ended questions and very carefully listen to customers and their unique responses. I often ask permission to take notes and the prospect really appreciates my personal interest.

L isten for the opportunities where your product or services would best benefit the prospective customer.

E xamine with the prospect how these benefits would best be serviced by your product or service by again utilizing open-ended questions. Remember, nobody likes to be told (or sold) anything. ("Telling isn't selling.")

S uccess in sales is derived from the rewards received through customers' ongoing—often lifetime—satisfaction.

effective salesperson has to constantly and consistently practice effectively listening. You need to sharpen your listening skills and make it a firm part of who you are as a person.

Damage From Not Listening

I'd like to share two situations I observed recently.

In the first instance, an insurance salesperson made the initial contact with a prospect and secured an appointment. The salesperson was clearly excited about the company's products. At their first appointment, immediately following introductions, the salesperson started forcefully recommending a certain product.

How on earth could that salesperson know what product to recommend without first conferring with the prospect about the prospect's existing portfolio? Where was this salesperson's knowledge about a proper fit between the prospect's portfolio and the recommended product?

A similar unfortunate incident occurred when I accompanied a friend to the dentist.

I sat in the waiting room while my friend was back with the dentist. Minutes later, my friend, looking frantic, appeared in the waiting room, hastily grabbed my arm, and pulled me out of the dentist's office.

What had happened? The dentist had said that my friend had three bad teeth and that he (the dentist) was going to pull them. My friend was against any pulling out of teeth (especially his own!) and, once calmed down, explained the situation. In a nutshell:

". . . I can't get through to customer service, your company is billing me for products I didn't order, your product doesn't . . ."

"So, how about I put you down for six more?"

- The dentist did not take the time to explain the entire situation and listen to my friend's concerns.
- The dentist did not take the time and care in explaining the options and listening to my friend's reactions to these options.
- It appeared that the dentist was set to pull out my friend's teeth right there and not allow my friend to voice any questions or concerns.

Active-Listening Skills

Being a good listener is not like being a properly tuned microphone or recorder. Active listening involves more than hearing what is said. It includes understanding and encouraging. A great listener draws people out for greater understanding. To be an active listener, practice these behaviors:

- Use nonverbal signals of interest and acceptance. Lean forward, nod, smile, and make eye contact.
- Give verbal signals. Say "uh hum," grunt, say "oh," and so forth.
- Restate what the speaker has said in your own words. Sometimes brief points can be restated directly.
- If there are problems, acknowledge them if

they are due to you, highlight them if they suggest a need.

It's hard to be a great listener because we can all process words far faster than others can speak. Use the extra time to work at active listening. You'll stay more involved with the conversation. And your customers will feel more rapport with you. Many people don't have a good audience to listen to them. They may want a relationship with you just to have someone with whom they can truly talk!

Listeners as Helpers

Think about how often we seek out assistance from people who are proven professionals in their areas of expertise. We seek out this type of an individual because we, as customers, desire credible and valid information, products, and services.

How do you think this credibility and validity is established?

Through your acquired reputation as an effective listener, not someone who is ready to push and sell anything. You only offer something when it meets my needs as a customer.

5 Key Factors for Better Listening

Here are five things to concentrate on to make yourself a better listener.

1 **Slow down and listen.** What is this person really trying to say?

2 **Watch for body language cues.** What are this person's body movements and reactions really telling me? Are this person's body movements telling me something different than the words they are expressing?

3 **Look at facial expressions and eyes.** What additional information can you discern about people by observing their facial expressions and eye movements?

Look at other person
I dentify information
S peak only in turn
T hink about what is being said
E motions—check them
N ever interrupt
—Robert Montgomery, *Memory Made Easy*

4 **Practice delaying your responses and reactions to what you hear.** Yes, that's right, bite your tongue! Focus on the messages this person is really trying to convey.

5 **To obtain even more information, practice using active-listening questions**—open-ended questions that help reveal even more about what this person is trying to express. What questions could you ask that begin with what, where, when, who, or how? (Remember to use "why" questions carefully so you don't sound accusing.)

Daily, practice taking a genuine and sincere interest in what others are saying to you. Make whatever they are saying to you the most important subject at hand (*not* whatever you have to say).

Remember:
- Slow down and Listen
- Collect your thoughts and Listen
- Listen and become part of your clients' and prospects' lives

THE POWER OF LISTENING

If questions are the key to consultative, relationship-oriented selling, then listening skills are the key ring. No matter what profession or job we are in, we are all trying to sell or convey a product, a service, or even an idea. Where we oftentimes fall short is by thinking first of ourselves.

What is best for the other individual comes first. Keeping the other person in mind is the most critical paradigm shift we as salespeople need to make today and for the future. This book is part of the needed shift. This paradigm shift is the one key element that is going to unlock the door to the "Lost Art of Listening" and expose the wondrous mysteries that effective listening has to offer.

10 Attributes of Effective Listening in Sales

Effective listening . . .

1. is an attitude.
2. motivates others.
3. enhances believability.
4. inspires individuals.
5. leaves few unanswered questions.
6. leaves little room for misjudgments.
7. enhances long-term closes.
8. places the POWER in the salesperson's hands.
9. sparks imagination for the seller and buyer.
10. makes sales fun.

Effective listening transforms salespeople into coaches, counselors, movers and shakers of their industries, trusted representatives of their missions, and approachable individuals in many aspects of their lives.

I have traveled across the U.S. and in other countries conducting workshops and presenting keynote addresses on "effective listening." I've discovered the number one roadblock to effective listening. It is that we are always getting ready with our next response to what the other person is saying or isn't saying.

Whatever we are getting ready to say or do eventually blurts out. The line of communication is cut and the exchanging of ideas concerning sales—or anything else—is stopped.

BARRIERS TO EFFECTIVE LISTENING

Certain human obstacles keep popping up to destroy or sidetrack the most well-intentioned listening efforts. I'd like to help you be aware of these barriers, so they don't get in the way of any new positive listening initiatives you will be pursuing.

Attitude

Keeping and maintaining an open mind while listening is essential in your being able to understand the total picture. If you only have part of the total information to assist your client, how do you know the solution you are offering is the correct one?

If you are carrying any prejudices or hostilities against anyone, they directly influence your ultimate solution for the client. Furthermore, if you have a negative attitude, it will be expressed in the way you listen and in the questions you ask of your client.

Stress

A mind void of as many distractions as possible—including stress issues—will help in acquiring the sale and in keeping a lifetime client. By listening hard, you can actually forget yourself and your stresses. Concentrate on understanding not only the words, but the situation and motivations behind the words, both of the speakers and their companies.

Keep in mind that stress, if not properly managed, will affect far more than your listening and sales. Without managing your own stress issues, your recommendations to your customer are likely to be inferior because stress inhibits your full understanding of the situation.

If you enjoy interacting with customers and prospects, these interactions can actually lower your stress from other sources.

Self-Centeredness

Salespeople are all too often ready with a solution, recommendation, or answer before the total situation is known. And, just as often in response, the clients or prospects immediately respond with a "no." These salespeople then typically respond with a defensive reaction.

What started this unhappy cycle? The self-centered salesperson was too anxious to offer a

> You'll invariably find the answers—if your ears are open. The average salesperson is a better talker than listener . . . . Listening is not enough. You have to let go of preconceptions and hear old laments as if for the first time.
> —Tom Peters

"My son, the meaning of life is clear . . . if you know how to listen."

Listening Pays Off

Leaders at Facilities Management, a $10 million contractor, were concerned that their salespeople were selling customers more than they needed. The company created a listening training program based on Stephen Covey's rule to "Seek first to understand, then to be understood." They credit the program with securing a multimillion contract because their people asked better questions and were able to tailor the proposal to exactly what the customer wanted.

solution (and close the sale) before all the information about the situation was revealed. Great listening skills take you out of yourself. You already know what you know. Take some extra time to be sure that you know what your prospects and customers know.

If you've positioned yourself correctly, the customer sees you as a potential expert resource in your field. Only when you have exhausted all avenues of effective listening with the customer will you be seen as centered on the customer, as a professional help source, consultant, and advisor in the customer's arena.

THE BENEFITS OF LISTENING

Remember the insurance customer who was instantly offered one product to cure all of his ills? Well, that person is now with a credible consultant team that handles a number of different vehicles for investing, saving, and retirement. This team meets quarterly with the individual and reviews the diversified portfolio originally created after several weeks of investigation. They continue to modify the investments for the client's lifetime benefits and for the client's children and grandchildren.

Remember my friend with his unfortunate trip to the dentist. In this case, my friend was still in pain from his teeth. He agreed to visit another dentist recommend by a friend of his who has been a happy patient for several years. This dentist examined my friend's teeth, provided x-rays, and had two other dental specialists in the same building do independent exams that day. Two days later, my friend met again with the new dentist and went over the options that the three dentists had agreed were appropriate. My friend accepted one of the recommended approaches and began treatment. My friend now goes to this new dentist every six months and is pleased with their doctor-patient relationship.

CONCLUSION

True sales success comes from the foundation of good *listening*. And listening itself is evolutionary. You start at one level and make changes as the relationship develops. Your level of listening evolves as trust and the relationship evolve.

Buyers aren't about to be *sold* any products or services. Buyers will purchase those products or services when they have established in their own minds a need that justifies such purchases. As has been said in other chapters, you don't sell, you help people buy. It's through the power of effective listening that the sale and the relationship evolve.

Salespeople of the 21st century will be listeners first, and talkers second. They will initially say very little about their offerings.

Sales will come from strategically planned listening approaches. These will revolve around the salesperson's listening to all the facts and

---

Goals For Your Listening

In marketing and sales, the acronym USP stands for Unique Selling Proposition. For listening, use the USP to represent Understanding, Solutions, and Personalization of listening goals.

UNDERSTANDING
Listening to:
- understand
- support
- open up a relationship
- show you care

SOLUTIONS
Listening to:
- offer assistance
- give value, substance and solutions
- help develop and close the sale

PERSONALIZATION
Listening to:
- grow a relationship
- uncover unique needs and wants
- appreciate others

Listen While You Work

Motorola had been working on landing a sale with a Hungarian telecommunications company for years, but hadn't been successful.

Motorola then decided to adopt an approach called "Solution Selling" that is much like consultative selling. Rather than push their line of products, they practiced listening to understand the true needs and frustrations of their customers.

It took a year to find that the customer was more interested in service and relationship than simply the technology. Their changed sales approach landed a $100 million dollar order.

—Rick Crandall, *1001 Ways to Market Your Services: Even If You Hate to Sell*

responses rather than stating everything there is to be known about the product or service.

The day of discovering, coaching, and helping clients has arrived. The day of the consultant/advisor is here. The high-pressure, information toting, and deceiving salesperson is now a dinosaur.

To be successful, keep these maxims in mind:

- Be a facilitator of ideas.
- Be an encourager.
- Be an advisor/consultant.
- Be a caring individual.
- Be a lifetime help source in your area of specialization.
- Be a person interested in others' needs first.
- *Be a listener.*

EXPLODE INTO ACTION

"Mere dreaming accomplishes nothing."
—John Wanamaker, department store pioneer

(1) Analyze your listening skills and decide which skills need to be improved.

(2) Practice active-listening techniques such as restatement.

(3) Write several open-ended questions appropriate for your customers' industries.

(4) Practice nonverbal listening skills like nodding, leaning forward, and saying "uh huh."

(5) Practice pausing before you speak.

(6) Know your facts well so that you don't have to
be deciding what to say while the customer is
speaking.

HOW TO DEAL WITH THE LONG BUYING CYCLE IN BUSINESS-TO-BUSINESS SELLING

Aldonna R. Ambler

Aldonna R. Ambler, CMC, CSP, is a growth strategist. The CEO of the international firm, AMBLER Growth Strategy Consultants, Inc., Ms. Ambler has specialized in the strategic needs of growth oriented companies for 27 years. Dozens of her clients now appear on lists of the fastest growing privately held corporations. Some of her clients include Northern Telecom, Pacific Bell, Chilton Publishing, Bank One, Scott Paper, Resorts International, Caesar's Casino, Habitat for Humanity, and the Business Technology Association.

An award-winning entrepreneur in her own right, she provides keynote speeches on "Breaking Through the Barriers to Growth" and "Taking Your Business to the Next Level." Ms. Ambler was the tenth person in the world to achieve professional certifications for both management consulting and professional speaking.

An active leader in the business community and an advocate for economic development, Ms. Ambler chaired The New Jersey delegation for the most recent White House Conference on Small Business, and has provided testimony at Congressional hearings.

Aldonna R. Ambler, CMC, CSP, 3432 Reading Avenue, Hammonton, NJ 08037-8008; phone (609) 567-9777 or (888) ALDONNA; fax (609) 567-3810; e-mail Aldonna@AMBLER.com.

HOW TO DEAL WITH THE LONG BUYING CYCLE IN BUSINESS-TO-BUSINESS SELLING

Aldonna R. Ambler

Generally, the higher the price of the product, the longer the sales cycle.

—Tony Alessandra et al., *Non-Manipulative Selling*

Business-to-business salespeople frequently complain that they face long buying cycles. This is especially true when it takes time to build relationships and establish trust. Long sales cycles not only delay your return on investment, but also increase uncertainty about whether the sale will go through at all.

WHY PROSPECTS DON'T BUY NOW

We all face four major challenges when we sell products or services to today's busy executives:

1 **It's just more work.** Prospects often view the purchase of a major service or product as another task in which they must invest their mental energy and due diligence.

2 **They're not sure what they're getting.** If you are selling services, you are essentially selling time, concepts, words—intangibles. To the prospective customer, that can feel like "air." Where are the measurable results? The guarantees?

3 **You're just one of a crowd.** Many direct competitors have well trained, talented salespeople, so your capacity to present benefits instead of features is no longer the distinguishing factor it once was.

4 **Prospects face too many other priorities.** The greatest challenge is that your real competition does not come from direct competitors. It is the myriad of other priorities that face your overworked prospective customers. Unless you can link what you offer to an "A" priority they already recognize, prospects won't take the time to think about you.

MANAGING THE BUYING CYCLE

What can you do when the buying cycle stretches longer and longer as your prospects decide to do other projects before even considering what you have to offer?

Your prospect may be a top priority to you, but it's likely that you are not a top priority for your prospect. To more quickly move through the buying cycle, try to link what you offer to one of their "A" priorities.

Prospect's Priority List

A Priorities
* Hire new office manager
* Decrease waste on production line
* Improve quality in Shipping Dept. to reduce returns

B Priorities
* Prepare quarterly report for boss
* Do paperwork for upcoming employee evaluations

C Priorities
* Archive old files
* Develop new supplier

YOU!

The Buying Cycle Starts With Your Marketing

It is important not to jump right into selling, but instead start with your marketing.

Market research can help you identify those companies that are more likely to have reached points in their development where they need what you offer. This knowledge can save you money on your marketing programs.

Effective marketing can help overcome the most important challenge—getting the attention of preoccupied decision makers. With a good marketing program, your marketing messages run alongside the lives of harried business people and remind them to think of your company when they are ready to consider that purchase.

An integrated marketing program uses the right methods to reach your prospects repeatedly. When your prospects participate in associations, your marketing messages are there as you participate right along with your busy prospective customers. When they attend conferences, your marketing messages are there in the form of speeches or seminars. When they attend their industry trade shows, your marketing messages are there with them in the form of exhibits, samples, or advertising specialties. When they are reading their industry publications, your marketing messages are there in the form of articles or display advertisements. When they sort their mail, your marketing messages are there in the form of newsletters, postcards, or invitations to special events. When they go on the Internet, your marketing messages are there in the form of Web pages, links, discussion forums, and directory listings.

What Is Integrated Marketing?

Integrated marketing is the practice of using many marketing methods to reach prospects multiple times with a single unified message.

Your marketing messages put you there with your prospective customers. You *will* catch their attention—if your marketing messages are related to the topics that are on their minds at the time.

Include response mechanisms (addresses; phone, fax, and e-mail numbers) with your marketing messages so that prospects can reach you when they are ready. Anything that you can do to convey an impression that it is easy to do business with you will help the prospect get ready to consider your products or services sooner.

Demonstrate the Value of Your Products and Services to their Current Priorities

Prospects may erroneously conclude that it's more cost efficient to complete their current projects before spending time thinking about your product or service. With technology and markets moving so fast, that may be a risky assumption on their part. For example, it is often more efficient to consider the merits of several possible employee benefits than to review them one by one. If you sell employee benefits, you could help your prospective customers reduce their administrative costs by speaking up and not passively accepting their "not yet" responses.

Perhaps your prospects are even approaching their major purchases in the wrong sequence. Companies that start the process of purchasing computer hardware without first selecting their software come to mind. When you offer to work very fast and prevent problems for them, your helpfulness positions you more as a partner and less as an outsider. For example, a life insurance provider who explains how to fund a buy/sell agreement upon the death of a partner can prevent a world of problems for business partners.

ACTION = $
You make the sale when the prospect understands that it will cost more to do nothing about the problem than to do something about it.
—Ben Feldman
in *Sales Upbeat*

STAGES OF READINESS

Not Everyone Will Be Ready at the Same Time

In working to accelerate the sales cycle, remember that your prospects' quests to improve their companies did not start when you showed up. Many will not reach a point where your product or service is relevant to them for quite some time.

Products and services that have long buying cycles are frequently considered at key points in the development of an organization. Let's say you sell telephone systems. A start-up business may be receptive to a limited investment. They will need to review their communication systems again when they have a steady base of customers. When they grow to multiple locations, they will once again need to evaluate and consider new systems.

Timing plays a large role in business-to-business marketing. There is a *continuum of readiness* among prospective customers. Keep this in mind as you work to build relationships that fit each prospect. The following four stages of readiness can help you define and understand your prospects' mindsets:

> ## Develop Customers' Goals
>
> Edwin Bobrow realized that by being a consultant to his customers he could be more useful. He took this now standard approach one step further. He developed yearly goals and strategies for each customer. He kept his eye on customers' long-term goals, which helped them achieve what they wanted, thus making customers happy to work with him.
>
> —Rick Crandall, *1001 Ways to Market Your Services: Even If You Hate to Sell*

- **Preoccupied.** At this stage, your prospects are so preoccupied with their current priorities that they will not notice your networking, seminars, exhibits, articles, advertisements, newsletters, and Web sites.

- **Not-Yet.** This group of prospective customers might be interested in what you have to offer, but they need more time to "come out from under" their current obligations. These prospects will want time to complete the major priorities that they currently have in motion before being asked to take on anything new.

- **Considering.** These prospects are considering adding the evaluation of your product or service to their next group of priorities. If your marketing messages have been consistent, these prospective customers will have paused to listen or read your messages, and may have kept a few of your marketing items.

- **Ready.** These prospective customers recognize your topic as a high priority and are ready to discuss details. If your marketing messages have been in their language, you may even be the only company contacted when these prospects are ready to buy.

Preoccupied Prospects

If one type of prospect never seems to move past being Preoccupied, your marketing manager should review your company's databases for accuracy. Maybe these people are not real prospects. If they are, it is usually a good idea to make sure that your company's marketing messages have been presented in the prospects' language. If the prospects are in an industry that your organization wants to serve, focused market research can uncover what is important to these prospects. Your

Use Technology to Keep in Touch and on Top

Contact management products like *ACT!, Telemagic, Sharkware,* and *GoldMine* can sort your prospects by industry, geographic location, the date of last contact, and other characteristics.

We also use ours to classify our prospects by readiness stage.

marketing message or methods may need to be revised based on the findings.

Not-Yet Prospects

Not-Yet prospects have noticed at least some of your marketing messages. If you respect their priorities, they may even talk with you about potential work "down the road." Use a marketing maintenance program for this group. You're hoping that when these Not-Yet prospects are ready to act, they will let you know. However, realistically, you'll need to keep tabs on their progress. This is a relationship-building stage for the salesperson.

Like all relationship-oriented sales situations, these prospects may not be ready to consider you because they really don't feel comfortable with you. Don't push. They may be stalling in order to test your persistence or sincerity, and to give themselves time to get comfortable with you.

Considering Prospects

Considering prospects accept you as a possible vendor. Keep your focus on moving from vendor status to consultant or advisor (see Chapter 2). Unless you have a clear unique selling proposition, you'll need to focus on building trust to differentiate yourself from competitors. Helping prospects with other priorities when there's no benefit to you is an important relationship-building technique that will be covered later in this chapter (and in other chapters).

Identify the concerns of these prospects and you will have a head start over your competitors. Ask Considering prospects to tell you one thing that makes the transition from their current priorities difficult for them. Armed with that knowledge, you can start working on solving that problem for them. Prospects gain the value of your problem-solving skills. Plus, when you are ready to communicate your solution to that problem, you have another opportunity to accelerate the sales process.

An example of helping prospects solve problems is Southern New England Telephone's 12-year cosponsorship of the SUCCESS Symposium series of seminars for small businesses. Southern New England Telephone (SNET) has attracted 33 straight sellout crowds. In addition to the goodwill that the seminars generate, the programs give SNET opportunities to develop relationships with owners of Connecticut's small businesses before they make important decisions about local, long distance, or Internet services.

Ready Prospects

Once you have the attention of a prospective customer, apply classic sales skills such as listening (see Chapter 8), emphasizing benefits over features, tailoring services to their particular situation, and so forth. If you've built a solid relationship, "closing" will involve mutual problem solving in an atmosphere of cooperation. Remember—closing the sale is simply the opening of the serious relationship. You don't want to revert back to old-fashioned, hard-sell methods that may get one sale at the cost of the long-term relationship.

Get Your Prospects to Sell You

When prospects trust you and want to work with you, spend time "training" them to sell you to other decision makers in their organizations. Internal contacts can help you build relationships with other influencers, but your key contact may still have to sell you to others.

WHERE DOES YOUR COMPANY FIT?

A Mutual Selection Process

In the final analysis, you can't force anyone to move up the buying continuum. You can only invite them to move more quickly by building trust and demonstrating value and sincerity. By the time the first order is closed, it should be anticlimactic—just a minor offshoot of a more central relationship.

At the same time that prospects are coming to trust you, you must evaluate their suitability as long-term clients. Replace prospect groups who aren't moving up the readiness continuum with another target industry or type of business that might at least move from Preoccupied to Not-Yet more quickly.

When NOT to Ask for the Business

Traditional sales training says to ask for the order "early and often." But when the prospect isn't in a buying mode, this brands you as a vendor, not a potential consultant or trusted advisor.

CAUTION

PROSPECT
NOT IN
BUYING
MODE

Sometimes, you will do best in seemingly unrelated industries. For example, the approach of my growth-strategy consulting firm seems to best match the needs of high-tech communication companies, family-owned businesses, professional service firms, and distributors. My venture capital firm has the best fit within service industries like hospitality and electronic bulletin boards. When I started, I didn't know that these industries would prove the most profitable.

HELPING PROSPECTS MOVE UP THE BUYING CONTINUUM

Use the following techniques to help prospects move up the readiness continuum.

Improve Coordination Between Marketing and Sales

CUSTOMER
READY
CONSIDERING
NOT-YET
PREOCCUPIED

The best way to move a Not-Yet prospect to the Considering stage is to have good coordination between your marketing and sales efforts. Without coordination, you will miss opportunities. Marketing people will assume that the salespeople are handling something while the salespeople assume that it is being handled by the marketing department. When prospects fall between the cracks, nobody benefits.

Handling Considering Prospects

Paint a picture of a brighter future. When prospects are just beginning to seriously consider you, they may not have a complete view of the benefits. Not only will they need information, but they will need your help to imagine their future . . . a future that is better because you are there. Most business-to-business salespeople could learn from fashion designers who send computer-generated photographs of their prospects wearing beautiful gowns in glamorous places.

Accept a boost from a strong friend. You may know someone who has the ear of your prospect. When prospects are not ready to talk with you, they may be open to listening to someone else. For instance, motivational keynote speaker Micki Williams landed a major account by asking five of her most prominent customers to make phone calls to a prospect.

Use transition campaigns. My growth-strategy consulting

Get a Sponsor

Formal sponsorships by others encourage prospects to move more quickly from Not-Yet to Considering to Ready. Over the years, I have benefited from being sponsored by *Entrepreneurial Edge* magazine, various business associations, and Core States Financial Corporation.

firm has successfully utilized transition campaigns to advance Not-Yet prospects to Considering status. Instead of emphasizing the benefits of our services—which the Not-Yet prospects have said they are not yet ready to consider—a transition-marketing campaign conveys three messages:

- genuine interest in prospects' current priorities
- an explanation of the connection between their current priorities and our normal area of focus
- ways to ease the transition from their current priorities to consideration of our services

You want prospects to view these transition marketing messages as a free service because they have been helped rather than pushed.

You can convey transition messages via mass marketing techniques (and not feel prematurely forced to do more expensive one-on-one selling). Research what is going on in your prospects' industries. There are priorities that prospects predictably face prior to considering your products or services. Once you know the typical patterns, you can have transition messages ready to send in the form of reprints of published articles, direct mail pieces, or e-mail. Prospects feel affirmed when they see articles about their exact situations, and prospects recognize and value your understanding of their situations.

Become a resource for quality referrals. Sometimes your prospects' priorities that must be met before purchasing your products or services are dramatically different from the solutions you offer. In this case, familiarity with firms that provide those solutions can help

Offer a Discount for Buying Sooner

Prospects often incur costs when they accelerate their processes to buy before they would otherwise have been ready. If you can establish a feeling of partnership, they may deserve some price consideration for changing their plans for you.

Price cutting is dangerous if prospects see you only as a vendor. But the costs of acquiring the account may be much less for your company if you get the prospect to make a decision sooner. Plus, your offer of a discounted price could reduce the field of potential providers and markedly decrease your costs associated with competing against several others.

EARLY ACCEPTANCE DISCOUNT

speed movement up the readiness continuum while establishing you as a helpful consultant.

My firm's interactions with Not-Yet prospects have become decidedly more productive because when prospects say they are "wrapped up in other priorities," we believe them. When you aren't busy trying to convince prospects to do something else, you can more comfortably shift to a conversation about their current priorities. Positioned as a source of constructive assistance, we can make solid referrals for other specialized services. For instance, because distributors are one of our target industries, we keep up on ECLIPSE and other brands of inventory-management software. Distributors return our calls when we phone to check on how their major investments in computer hardware and software have worked out— because we've helped them.

Expanding your products and services to address prospects' priorities that typically come before yours. Although this is not the first option to consider, my company has sped up prospect readiness by broadening our range of services to address prospects' needs that tend to take priority over use of our core services. Accounting firms that create departments to select and install new computer systems for their prospects and clients are an example of this approach. Once these firms have established a working relationship with a client about their computers, the move up the readiness continuum regarding their accounting services proceeds faster. The firm that provides both computer and accounting-related services usually has a head start over competitors that only provide accounting services.

Low-Risk Samples

Sometimes you can offer simpler, safer services or products that become ways to make it safe for people to try you out at low risk. For instance, offer inexpensive "analysis" services to assess needs. The prospect gets a low-cost service and you get your foot in the door. (See also Chapter 4 on needs analysis.)

BUILD RELATIONSHIPS WHILE YOU WAIT

One indirect benefit of longer sales cycles is that you have more time to build rapport with prospects. Whatever techniques you use to try to accelerate the sales cycle, make sure you don't harm the potential long-term relationship. Repeat business is where the major profits lie. The first sale is only your starting point.

Take the opportunity to learn more about your prospects. When service providers misinterpret "not yet" as "no," they miss opportunities to get to know their prospective customers. Sometimes prospective customers do not realize that they are revealing important information when they discuss priorities that do not directly relate to our core services. We can learn how they view vendors, if they are organized, if they are logical and fair, what is important to them, how fast they move, how their decisions are made, and so forth. This information can come in very handy when it's your turn to submit a proposal.

Start treating the prospect like a customer. We have found that it's a good idea to add Considering prospects to our distribution list for some of the special services that are offered to our clients. It's relatively easy to include prospects in book discount programs, special newsletters, referral services, online chat sessions, and seminars. Several of our clients have created "Friends Of" programs to begin providing special incentives for their prospects while maintaining strong client-only programs. Simple gestures like inviting a

---

Repeat-Customer Value

Taco Bell has determined that a repeat customer is worth about $11,000 in lifetime total sales. At Sewell Cadillac, that figure is $332,000. Xerox has learned that a *very satisfied customer* is six times more likely to repurchase Xerox equipment than a merely *satisfied* customer. A recent study found that reducing customer defections by just 5% resulted in an 85% profit increase in a bank's branch system; a 50% profit increase in an insurance brokerage; and a 30% increase in an auto service chain.

—*Achieving Breakthrough Service,*
Harvard Business School

prospective client to attend a Chamber of Commerce function with you can speed up their movement from Considering to Ready.

Spread your contacts. The prospects who have told you that they are busy and cannot consider your products or services at this time may not be the only persons involved with buying decisions. It pays to send information about your products and services to an expanded group of people within prospect companies. Someone else may not be quite as preoccupied. For example, office equipment salespeople who first pitch their products to me do much better if they figure out that their future calls and literature should be directed to our office manager.

Build credibility in their eyes. Not-Yet prospects like to be remembered but not pestered. Sending a copy of an article relevant to their situation will be appreciated, but keep the cover note short. If your name is in front of them, it's more likely that they will think of you when they move up to Ready.

RECOGNIZE THE VALUE OF HAVING PROSPECTS FROM ALL FOUR CATEGORIES

Salespeople sometimes fantasize about having only Ready prospects in their contact management systems. But if prospects came to you ready to buy, you wouldn't have the time to get

Marty Abo, Everywhere You Look

An accountant I know, Marty Abo, CPA, has an incredible knack for getting positive media coverage. He serves on the board of directors for a local bank. He chaired the small business action committee for the Chamber of Commerce of Southern New Jersey, and he recently won an SBA award as New Jersey's Accountant Advocate. He even got publicity in the lifestyle section of the local paper when he went to the 25th-anniversary Woodstock outdoor concert.

When previously preoccupied prospects within Southern New Jersey start to think about changing accountants, they can't help but think about Marty Abo because they will have seen his name in the newspaper so many times.

Not-Yet Prospects

Most companies spend about 90% of their marketing budget on producing sale leads—but only 10% to follow up on them. Other studies show that about 26% of inquirers say they will buy within six months, 56% say they will buy eventually, and 18% have no plans to purchase, according to Wilson & Associates.

Over the long term, the group that plans to buy later produces four times more buyers than the 26% who say they'll buy soon. If people say they plan to buy later, keep in touch and use the extra time to build the relationship.

—*Executive Edge* newsletter

to know each other. Without the foundation of a solid relationship, how could you differentiate yourself from other vendors? Ready prospects would largely be price shoppers dealing with commodities. That's not where you want to be.

Ready prospects can slip down the continuum to Considering when you least expect it. If you haven't been working with Considering prospects, you may miss cues or not understand what is important to people who have not yet found time for you. Similarly, Preoccupied prospects can suddenly advance to Ready. You would not want to lose accounts merely because you were out of touch with these prospects. The most successful salespeople I know work on all four groups simultaneously to keep their sales pipelines flowing.

Relationship Readiness

Looking at your prospects along a continuum of readiness will be a good parallel as you look at them along a relationship-building continuum. The two will move together closely. But each will give you ideas on how to behave to enhance the relationship and the likelihood and speediness of the sale.

Tracking the movement of your prospects along the readiness continuum will help you tailor your messages, see what is working, feel a sense of progress, focus on long-term relationships, and build momentum. All of these actions will help you produce to more sales.

BURST INTO ACTION

"Great thoughts put into practice become great acts."

—William Hazlett

(1) Coordinate your marketing and sales efforts. Communicate regularly with prospects and research their industries.

(2) Use integrated marketing to *be there* when your prospect begins to move along the readiness continuum. Use different approaches to reach major prospects, but make sure your marketing materials have the same look and give the same key messages.

(3) Research how what you sell fits with the other priorities of your prospects. List ways to tie what you do to their higher priorities. Develop a list of referral sources for related products and services.

(4) Classify your prospects into the Preoccupied, Not-Yet, Considering, and Ready stages of the readiness continuum. Add this data to your contact management files.

(5) Understand prospects' purchasing needs so you can help them with their buying processes as an objective consultant.

(6) Help customers track their long-term goals in your area—possibly even help develop the goals for your customers.

(7) With Preoccupied prospects, review your data base, spread your contacts, and look for targets that will move faster along the readiness continuum.

(8) With Not-Yet prospects, don't push. Build your credibility by improving the coordination between your marketing and sales efforts; use transitional campaigns; provide help even when there's no clear benefit to you; and take the opportunity to learn more about your prospects.

(9) With Considering prospects, focus on moving from vendor to advisor status. Paint a picture of a brighter future that includes your help. Start treating the prospect like a customer.

(10) With Ready prospects, tailor your products and services, emphasize benefits over features, and remember that Ready prospects can slip back to Considering at any time. Focus on the long-term relationship and resist regressing back to old fashioned, high-pressure closing techniques.

Chapter 10

THE CONSULTATIVE PRESENTATION

John W. Hobart

John W. (Buddy) Hobart
is the founder and president of
Solutions 21, a company that
provides customized training
programs and strategic planning services. Mr. Hobart and Solutions 21 have
conducted seminars and training programs on consultative sales strategies, and
presentation skills. Offices are located in Pittsburgh and Phoenix. Programs have
been successfully customized and implemented for clients as diverse as *Inc. 500*
and *Fortune 500*, and range from professional services firms to manufacturing
plants. Mr. Hobart's ideas have been used successfully in such companies as
Pfizer, USX, Lanier Worldwide, Coopers & Lybrand, Eckerd Health Services,
KPMG Peat Marwick, and American International. Solutions 21 has presented
programs on four continents with participants representing 22 countries.

Prior to starting Solutions 21, Mr. Hobart served as the general manager
for a major office equipment dealer in the Northeast. While there, his office
produced five times the industry average in strategic product sales and twice the
industry average in bottom-line profits.

In addition to his work at Solutions 21, Mr. Hobart is a frequent speaker
at universities, business forums, and conventions. He is the author of *Hire
Education*.

John "Buddy" Hobart, Solutions 21, 912 Washington Avenue, Pittsburgh, PA 15106;
phone (412) 429-2121; fax (412) 429-5242; www.solutions-21.com.

THE CONSULTATIVE PRESENTATION

John W. Hobart

"Presentations and proposals are a great place to
confirm your relationship progress."

—Rick Crandall,
1001 Ways to Market Your Services: Even If You Hate to Sell

The presentation is a key component of the
consultative sales process for the first sale. During
this meeting, if all goes well, a new partnership is
formed and the salesperson leaves not having just
closed the order, but having opened a long-term
relationship.

Yet, after working hard to set themselves
apart from their competitors, many salespeople
ease up when it comes to the presentation. They
rationalize that the presentation is a mere formal-
ity—after all, aren't building rapport and trust,

understanding the account's needs, and devising creative or unique solutions, more important than a presentation? All that is needed at this point is to communicate the solution to the decision maker . . . right?

Wrong! With your presentation, you can communicate the solution, reinforce your expertise and professionalism, *and* open the long-term relationship. A consultative presentation will either confirm your "value added" or open you up to additional objections and further scrutiny as a common vendor.

Ask yourself, "When it comes to the presentation, do I 'come to play?'" Successful consultative sales professionals always come to play. They realize that the presentation can create new challenges. Expert consultative sales professionals have learned to recognize, prepare for, and defuse each possible problem.

> A consultant's problem-solving approach to selling requires helping customers improve their profits, not persuading them to purchase products and services . . . . The ideal positioning for a consultative seller is *customer profit improver.*
> —Mack Hanan, *Consultative Selling*

FOUR ISSUES TO BE PREPARED FOR

Every presentation has four areas that must be dealt with.

1 Buyers experience cognitive dissonance. The consultative sales process can involve a phenomenon called cognitive dissonance.

All decision makers, including those of us in the sales profession, have a stereotype of the "typical" salesperson etched in their minds. In seminars around the world, I draw out of audiences the characteristics of typical salespeople. From Sydney to San Francisco, audiences always list similar negative characteristics. These stereotypes are reinforced and perpetuated in cartoons, jokes, TV, movies, and other media.

Salespeople who use consultative approaches break through the negative stereotypes and set themselves apart. But the act of buying can create

Dissonance Theory

Dissonance theory proposes that when people behave inconsistently with their attitudes, they experience an unpleasant state of arousal called cognitive dissonance. Psychologist Leon Festinger suggested two main ways people can reduce dissonance: They can change their behavior, or they can change their beliefs and attitudes.

—R.A. Lippa,
Introduction to Social Psychology

dissonance because the decision makers associate themselves with something they view negatively (salespeople).

A presentation can cause the decision maker to view you—the consultant—as a typical salesperson. Decision makers can become aggressive, critical, and overly challenging in order to alleviate their tensions.

During the presentation, any sign of typical salesperson behaviors (for example, lack of preparation or knowledge) can derail the entire relationship-building—and sales—process. If you display typical sales characteristics, decision makers will go out of their way to reach a negative cognitive judgment and break off the relationship.

2 **Buying is stressful.** During "official" presentations, you are not the only one under pressure. Decision makers also feel a great deal of stress. Making a decision, committing their company's resources, and managing the dissonance are all stress inducers. To get to this point, a good relationship had to be built, so the decision maker was more likely to be friendly, open, and helpful. Now, during the presentation, he or she may be agitated, withdrawn, argumentative, or critical. If others are present, decision makers may play to the audience, or step back to seem objective.

3 **A team often makes the purchase decision.** The decision-making process in organizations has changed dramatically over the past decade. Gone is the autocratic manager. Decisions are now likely to be made by a cross section of departments and individuals who may have very different agendas and personal styles.

If you are fortunate, you have been able to meet all of the key players during the sales process. More often than not, schedules do not allow for much in-depth interaction. Therefore, when it comes time to present a specific solution, you may choose to focus the presentation on the one individual or department with whom you are most familiar. The risk you run is alienating the other, possibly more influential, participants.

Sometimes, a salesperson *does not know* a decision will be made by a team. During my seminars, salespeople frequently tell me about new persons being added to the process at the last minute. It is not uncommon to have someone who has apparently had no involvement join a presentation meeting.

A good team is made up of individuals with complementary skillsets, personal styles, and points of view. By enlisting various points of view, a decision maker hopes to gain a balanced perspective. Many times a decision maker will take a back seat during the final presentation and allow the team to take control. Whenever a presenter is faced with more than one person in a meeting, the chance of competing agendas and styles is great. Failure to prepare for this contingency can doom the sale.

4 Tips for Better Presentations

- **If possible, stand up while you make your presentation.** This gives you a position of more authority and assertiveness.
- **Make eye contact.** This shows you are open to input.
- **Stay alert to nonverbal cues.** If your audience looks bored, do something different (for instance, ask a question of the audience or change slides).
- **Avoid qualifiers.** Putting "I think" or "I believe" before a statement weakens it. Your audience knows who is speaking. Compare:
  I think this system will save you money.
  This system will save you money.

4 **Listening takes energy, but is boring.** Salespeople mistakenly believe that they, and not the audience, are doing all of the work during a presentation. While presenting does take a great

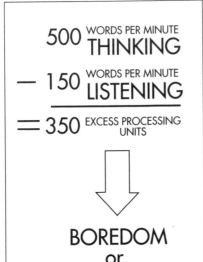

500 WORDS PER MINUTE
THINKING

— 150 WORDS PER MINUTE
LISTENING

= 350 EXCESS PROCESSING
UNITS

**BOREDOM
or
DAYDREAMING**

TIP: Don't let your audience get bored or daydream. See that they use those 350 excess processing units on your presentation. Stimulate your audience with questions, handouts, eye contact, and audience discussion.

deal of energy, so does listening. A presenter is there to have people *listen*, not just hear the words. Listening requires concentration, and concentration takes energy (see also Chapter 8).

The human brain can process about 500 words per minute. The average American speaks at 150 words per minute. This 350-word difference can cause "tune-out," allowing audience members' minds to wander. Studies have shown that people tend to misinterpret up to 70% of the verbal messages they receive. This may be attributed to the brain being understimulated with only 150 words a minute to process, and the mind tuning out portions of the message.

It is no wonder that so many people "flip to the last page" and look for a price during a proposal presentation. The human brain demands more information than it is receiving at 150 words per minute.

A presenter must fill the gap to fully engage the listener in order to maintain control of the presentation. The gap is not filled with words, but with other stimuli. Visual aids, proposal documents, and body language must all work in concert in order to fully engage the audience.

PRESENTING WITH STYLE

Closing the sale is a major goal of any sales presentation. However, goals like maintaining the audience's confidence in your expertise and enhancing the relationship are also important.

Bear in mind that your audience will have the tendency to stereotype you as being like most other salespeople. As a consultative salesperson, you must continually add value to the sale. Always present yourself as a professional and take care to not appear in any way typical. As a professional, you do not charge into a final presentation without proper preparation. Only amateurs wing it.

Just as there are four issues that can hurt presentations, there are four steps to giving successful presentations. Each step builds upon the prior one and, when used in concert, helps reduce cognitive dissonance, manages decision makers' stress, prepares for any team-member style, and helps people *listen* to the solution.

1 **Recognize style differences.** Much research has been done on how personal behavioral styles influence an individual's behavior in certain situations. Most classifications break behavioral styles into four main orientation categories: action, people, process, and detail oriented. While everyone uses each of the styles on occasion, people tend to use one or two orientations in most of their interactions.

Each style group reacts differently under pressure. Since buying and selling is stressful, and the sales presentation can be the *most stressful* step in the sales process, it is important for the consultative salesperson to understand the stress responses of each orientation.

Knowledge of these stress reactions should also be applied to yourself. Since you are also

---

Behavioral Styles' Reactions Under Pressure

Here are how the various styles typically react under pressure:

Detail-Oriented
Will demand details and be slow to make a decision.

Action-Oriented
Will become very impatient with the details and make demands to "get to the point."

Process-Oriented
Will require step-by-step approaches and will be resistant to change.

People-Oriented
Will want to talk about it and gain assurances that other people have been pleased with the results.

under pressure during the presentation phase, chances are that you will also revert to your natural tendencies. When this occurs, you may try to impose your style on the audience, regardless of their needs. If you do, you'll jeopardize the sale and the relationship.

2 **Include key elements in your consultative presentations and proposals.** The difference between a presentation and a proposal is that a proposal is usually written and a presentation is normally given in person.

Of course, the proposed solution to your prospects' problems should be included in every proposal and presentation. In addition, each presentation should contain these five additional elements:

- executive summary
- references
- implementation schedule
- back-up details
- extra copies of the proposal

The Executive Summary

Every consultative presentation should start with an executive summary. An executive summary is a review, *in the prospects' words*, of their needs and your conversations to date. This will provide a road map for the presentation and assure the audience that you will be addressing their needs, and not wasting their time. It is an important step in securing the complete confidence of your audience.

"I suggest you make your presentation as brief as possible."

An executive summary should contain six to ten points outlining your previous conversations. Each point should be no more than three sentences. If you have met with more than one person during the sales process, their concerns should also be addressed. The following is a list of effective openings to the points in an executive summary:

- During our last meeting, we discussed . . .
- You said your biggest challenge was . . .
- An area you said needs addressing is . . .
- Currently, you feel . . .
- A major consideration of ABC Company is . . .

By starting your presentation with an executive summary, you display your understanding of the issues addressed in the proposal. The executive summary acts as an agenda, and puts the audience at ease, since they know you understand their concerns and will be answering *their* issues. Finally, an executive summary helps to manage the audience's stress since it "connects" with all of the styles (more about presenting the executive summary on page 162).

Behavioral Styles. Each behavioral style will look for something different in the executive summary (and in the proposal). In each case, by using language that speaks to their particular style, you will connect better with them.

References

References should be included in each proposal and presentation. Do not simply provide company names you have worked with, but also include a contact name, address, and memorized phone number. Do not refer to

Create an Executive Summary that Communicates to All Behavioral Styles

Make sure your executive summary communicates with all of your audience's behavioral styles. Use the following techniques:

- **Detail-Oriented**
Present details in their words.

- **Action-Oriented**
Get to the point and do not introduce unnecessary details.

- **Process-Oriented**
Discuss only those points they want to address and do not suggest unnecessary changes.

- **People-Oriented**
Present in their words, thus showing you listened and have personalized the presentation.

Delivery Tips to Match Different Personal Styles

The following delivery tips will help you manage and connect effectively with the various behavioral styles in attendance.

Detail-Oriented

If there are any key numerical points or important dates in your proposal, memorize them. Do not use approximations if at all possible. By stating "our research shows you will receive a 4.85% increase . . ." versus "our research shows you will receive about a 5% increase . . ." you are displaying a mastery of the details. Approximate numbers will open you up to criticism from any detail-oriented member of the audience.

Action-Oriented

Speaking, not reading, your points and using the executive summary will help you connect with the action-oriented people in your audience. Use direct, results-oriented language, such as "you will see . . ." versus "we hope you see . . . ." This sets a "bottom line" tone. Be prepared to discuss the results you have achieved for others.

People-Oriented

Memorize the names and phone numbers of your references. Do not refer to "XYZ Company" but talk about "Mike Anthony at XYZ Company, his number is 555-1548." Talking about your references as human beings instead of impersonal organizations will create a sense of security for people-oriented individuals. Also, knowing the phone numbers will highlight the personal connection you have with your customers (as well as impress the detail-oriented).

Process-Oriented

Choosing the proper language is critical to put process-oriented people at ease. Do not refer to "problems to fix" but rather "issues that need to be addressed." Use your implementation schedule to highlight your ability to handle any "bumps in the road." Frequently, I hear consultants say something like "and, naturally, as with any new system you'll have some problems, but don't worry, we can handle them." The process-oriented person stops listening at the word "problem."

the company name first, but rather use the individual's name when discussing each reference—for example, "Tom Graylash at Henson & Sons can be reached at (555) 211-6842. We worked with him on . . . ."

Discussing the person versus the company helps the various styles feel more comfortable with you as a value-added consultant. Detail-oriented people will appreciate your mastery of the details (knowing the phone number). Action-oriented styles will want to know you have produced results for others. References will help process-oriented people realize others have made changes. And since you refer to the references by name and know their phone numbers, people-oriented styles will like the personal touch that it conveys.

Implementation Schedule

Process- and detail-oriented styles will respond to an implementation schedule in every presentation. An implementation schedule should be a step-by-step outline of how the proposal will be implemented. It will help alleviate the questions and concerns of any process/detail oriented-people. If no process/detail-oriented styles are a part of the audience, do not spend time on the schedule unless requested to do so. Action/people-oriented styles do not care as much about the details of an implementation schedule.

Back-up Details

Be sure to have all of the necessary details somewhere in

Sample Implementation Schedule

DATE	TOPIC
1/99	National Kickoff Meeting
3/99	Managers' Meeting: Change Management
4/99	Employee Program: Change Management
5/99	Managers' Meeting: Change Management/ Performance Management
6/99	Employee Program: Change Management/ Conflict Resolution
7/99	Managers' Meeting: Coaching and Counseling
8/99	Employee Program: Team Building
9/99	360-Degree Review
10/99	Final Report

> It has long been an axiom of mine that the little things are infinitely the most important.
>
> —Sherlock Holmes (Sir Arthur Conan Doyle)

the proposal. If additional detail is needed to support any of your claims, bring the data along, just in case it is asked for. Action-oriented and people-oriented individuals will not want to scour the material, but the process- and detail-oriented folks will want to see this back-up information.

As with the implementation schedule, do not address these details in your presentation unless answering a request for additional information. You conducted the research, included the information, and are prepared to offer details. But that may not be necessary. Simply proving you have the details may be all that is required.

Even if you are certain of your audience's style and think you will not need all of this information, include it anyway! Your proposal will represent you in your absence. Having all of these elements included will also increase your chances if or when the package is passed along for input from someone else.

It Pays to Be Prepared

Recently, my firm, Solutions 21, was consulting with a large school district on creating a "School to Work" program and curriculum. We had been working with the superintendent of the district on all of the preliminary details and were finally prepared to present the proposal.

The superintendent assured us she was the decision maker and would be the only one sitting through the final presentation.

When we arrived for the meeting, there were eight additional people in attendance, some of whom had just been asked to attend that morning! Since we were prepared with additional copies *and* had prepared for *any* style, our presentation was not negatively affected.

Extra Copies

Even if you have verified and reverified who will be attending, be prepared to adjust your presentation for last-minute additions. Having enough extra copies to leave behind for any size audience will enhance your image and show your preparation. Should your proposal need to be passed along for input, originals are much better than photocopies. Originals look professional and all of your hard work will not be ruined by poor copy quality.

3 **Be prepared for the unexpected.** As previously discussed, the final presentation often brings surprises and new challenges. It leaves little room for trial and error. Being prepared is the key to avoiding problems. Fortunately, the most important element of preparation is also the only element you completely control . . . yourself.

Learn more about yourself. Take a Myers Briggs or DiSC® Profile (or find the one you took years ago). Don't just look at the elements of your behavior that you already know . . . examine your developmental areas. Be open-minded and challenge your view of yourself.

A potential source of problems during a presentation is when someone "pushes your buttons." By knowing your own style, developmental areas, and behaviors under pressure, you will be able to better manage *yourself*. Your responses will be more appropriate and productive and less likely to be your high-stress, natural reactions.

Use Video

Self-understanding and self-management will make you less likely to sabotage your own presentations. But before charging ahead, put your new understanding to the test by videotaping yourself prior to any important presentation. Create a mock audience and have them challenge you with the "most feared" objections. Have them throw in a few off-the-wall comments. For example, if you are a detail-oriented person, have your test audience become frustrated with details. Or, if you are action-oriented, have them demand details.

The camera will not lie. Not only will it capture your words, but it will also reveal your body language and voice inflections.

Rules for Video Role Play

- Do not step out of the role play. During a live presentation you cannot call time-out.
- Do not "say what you will say." Say it *exactly* as you intend to at the actual meeting.

Do not video yourself from just one angle, but from various side angles as well. We seldom see ourselves from the side, and this information could be very revealing, especially if you will be presenting to more than one person.

Tape yourself using any support materials, slides, overheads, props, etc. that will be a part of your presentation. When reviewing the video, be sure you look comfortable and the transitions from one point to the next appear natural. The camera will simulate an audience and cause you to be a little nervous and self-conscious. What might *feel* natural may not *look* natural. The video will help you both feel and look more natural by letting you see yourself as others do and allowing necessary adjustments to be made prior to the meeting.

Express Yourself

Most people talk in more of a monotone than they realize. Grab a tape recorder and recite something into it. Get crazy with your intonation! Then play the tape back. You might find that it sounds pretty good.

—*Art Sobczak's Telephone Selling Report*

If a video camera and mock audience are unavailable, use the old standby . . . practice in front of a mirror. There is one twist to this tried-and-true method. Use a tape recorder while practicing. The mirror will give you a visual idea and the tape recorder will reveal voice inflection and your exact language. Listen to the tape and determine if what you actually said is exactly what you meant.

4 **Stand and deliver: Tips to enhance your presentation.** The final step to successfully avoid problems is to implement the tools we've been discussing. A consultative presentation must include several elements in order to be successful. Since people can listen faster than we speak, more senses must be engaged to fill the gap.

Use some type of media to complement the printed page or verbal presentation. Visual representations of your points will help the audience stay focused and will increase their retention.

Whether you are using multi media or a flip chart, use bullet points and *speak* the message. Do not read it word for word. The audience will be seeing the message visually, reading it to themselves *and* hearing you talk about it . . . all at the same time. By engaging more senses, you are increasing the rate of retention *and* helping the audience to listen more effectively.

> People retain only 10% of what they hear, but 50% of what they hear *and* see.
> —*3M News*

As previously mentioned, use the executive summary as an agenda for the presentation. Briefly discuss each point in order to gain agreement for the direction of the presentation. After you have reviewed all of the points, ask: "Has anything else surfaced since our last meeting that we will need to address in our proposal?"

If the answer is no, test the waters by asking something such as: "So, if we address each of these points to your satisfaction, will we have your blessing to move forward?"

If the answer is yes, ask: "What needs to be added?" Do not address each point yet, but keep asking: "Is there anything else?" until you are relatively sure you have uncovered all of the new points and issues. Decide where each point fits into your current structure and assure the audience you will discuss each during your presentation. This will give you time to formulate your responses and allow you to regain control of the presentation.

Many sales professionals find it difficult to ask for additional points at this stage out of fear of derailing the presentation before it begins. They avoid asking any tough questions up front, hoping that once they get started, their audience will forget any issues they had going into the presenta-

Gender Differences

Female speakers tend to not speak as forcefully as they should, and therefore seem less authoritative and convincing. Women should try breathing deeply and speaking more in a tone of command.

Men sometimes speak too seriously and in a monotone voice. They need to vary their pace and express more personality when they speak.

—S. Asher and W. Chambers, *Wooing and Winning Business*

tion. As a consultative salesperson, don't do this! More often than not, the audience will *not* forget their initial concerns, even if you addressed them during the course of your presentation. The reason is simple . . . they will not have been listening. Their minds will be on *their* issues and not on what you are saying. I call this the "coffee pot" syndrome.

Have you ever gone to work and once there, wondered whether you turned off the stove (coffee pot, iron, etc.) at home? All day you can't completely shake the thought from your consciousness. No matter what you're working on, the thought keeps popping up. As soon as you get home, you completely disregard your normal routine and go directly to the kitchen to see if it is turned on.

Including tough issues in an executive summary lets you turn off your audience's coffeepots. If they have issues they want addressed, they will be lodged in their minds throughout your presentation. Not only will this limit their ability to listen, it almost guarantees an objection at the end of your presentation. Whether you like it or not, they will go straight to their proverbial coffeepots, possibly derailing your entire presentation.

SUMMARY

I remember watching a track meet on television when I was a kid. It was the men's 400-meter finals, and the top finishers would qualify for the Olympics. As the runners in one heat approached the tape, one of them, believing he was far enough ahead of the others, threw his arms up in celebration before he crossed the finish line. He celebrated too early.

A runner right behind him drove through the finish line and beat him by the tiniest of margins. His celebration cost him the Olympics. He failed to give 100% until the end, and let up at the most crucial moment of his career.

As a consultative sales professional, presentations are one type of the many performances you need to concentrate on. Don't let up. Drive through the tape and ensure that all of your hard work to build relationships will be rewarded. A successful presentation does far more than "close" a sale. It opens up the future of your ongoing relationship with that client.

BURST INTO ACTION

"It's better to do something—even the wrong thing—than to do nothing at all."
—Thomas Watson, Jr., IBM

(1) Decide ways you can reduce the stress or dissonance of people who buy from you.

(2) Prepare material for people with different job responsibilities who might be on a buying team.

(3) Prepare material for different personality styles.

(4) Analyze your personal style. Decide how you can match up with different personalities.

(5) Work on managing your "hot buttons." Don't allow them to be pushed.

(6) Create visuals to complement your verbal points.

(7) Create tables which summarize data for the detail-oriented.

(8) If you want to improve your verbal presentation skills, go to a Toastmasters-type group locally.

(9) If you want to improve the readability of your written proposals, use shorter words, shorter sentences, and shorter paragraphs.

(10) Practice, practice, practice.

BRINGING IT ALL TOGETHER WITH A SYSTEM

Theodore W. Garrison III

Theodore W. Garrison III works with existing and start-up companies who want to grow their businesses. He helps individual companies directly, as well as through associations and organizations. His programs emphasize the need for innovation in areas of management, marketing, and sales.

Mr. Garrison has more than 25 years of business, leadership, and motivation experience working in the construction and real estate development industries. He has held executive positions involved with the design, construction, and marketing of almost a billion dollars worth of facilities, including hotels, office buildings, and public facilities. He has been a licensed real estate broker since 1981.

In 1994, he established Garrison Associates which provides seminars and keynote speeches for businesses and associations on management, marketing, and sales strategies. His talks are both informative and entertaining.

Garrison is a member of the National Speakers Association and the American Seminar Leaders Association. He is a co-author of the book *Marketing for People Not in Marketing.*

Theodore W. Garrison III, Garrison Associates, 900 W. Valley Road, Suite 201H, Wayne, PA 19087; phone (610) 341-8605; fax (610) 889-0901; e-mail garrison@bellatlantic.net.

BRINGING IT ALL TOGETHER WITH A SYSTEM

Theodore W. Garrison III

"You must create a system or be enslaved by another man's."

—William Blake

The earlier chapters discussed a philosophy and many specific ideas which can substantially improve your sales performance and income. However, even if you master each and every idea, you will not reach your full potential as a sales professional until you develop a sales system. (Or, if you are a sales manager, your sales department will not reach its full potential without a duplicable sales system.)

Those statements may appear bold, but they're true. Selling today is more complex than ever before, making a sales system essential to effectively manage the sales process. With today's highly competitive sales environment, a sales system is a requirement for top performance.

THE VALUE OF A SYSTEM

Can you make sales without a system? Certainly, but ask yourself the following questions:
- Will those sales maximize your personal sales potential?
- Will the return justify the effort and time required to close the transaction?
- Will those sales build your business over the long haul, or are they just one-time events?

If you're honest with yourself, the answers to first two are probably "no," and the answer to the third question is "one-time sales."

Study after study indicates that the most successful salespeople have developed a sales system (even if they call it something else).

An effective sales system is built on referrals and repeat customers because these are the most profitable sales. And, as this book has discussed, referrals and repeat sales can only be built by concentrating on the interests of the customer.

The newest approach to customer-focused selling is Don Peppers' and Martha Rogers' one-to-one marketing. In this approach, databases are used to focus on segments of one. Instead of targeting groups, the unique needs of the individual customer are targeted, with customers offered customized solutions. The de-

The Changing World of Marketing

Core truths about customers have changed drastically in the last five years. (1) There's a world of choice out there. People are looking for products they can trust, not just ones that meet their needs. (2) Customers want the suppliers to help them conserve time. Today, the gift of time must be an integral part of the added value of your product or service. (3) Instead of marketing to segments of the masses, we must market to segments of one.

—Lou Pritchett, *Stop Paddling and Start Rocking the Boat: Business Lessons from the School of Hard Knocks*

mands of handling prospects as individuals makes it even more crucial that the salesperson have a system to track all of the details.

WHAT DOES A SYSTEM DO?

A system is a process that produces predictable results. The late internationally renowned business consultant W. Edwards Deming said that the biggest crisis facing American business is the failure to develop processes that produce predictable results over and over again. Dr. Deming's comment was directed at every aspect of business, but here we will focus on the need for a sales system.

A sales system is merely a step-by-step procedure that insures that all of the necessary bases in the sales process are covered in order to increase your likelihood of consummating the sale. A system breaks down the relationship-building process of a complex sale into manageable parts. An appropriate analogy would be the construction of a large building. Both tasks are complex activities that require the use of a wide range of skills and techniques that must be accomplished in a specific order to obtain the desired results.

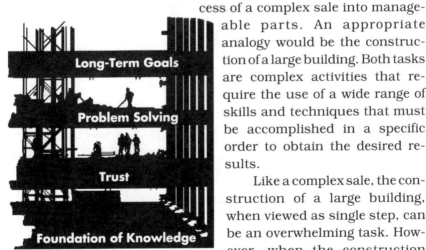

Like a complex sale, the construction of a large building, when viewed as single step, can be an overwhelming task. However, when the construction project is broken down into hundreds, if not thousands, of smaller tasks, the overall project becomes manageable. Preparing a schedule requires the identification of all the various tasks and then assigning each its proper place in the sequence of events. Often this process alone reveals potential problems that were not apparent when the project was looked at as a single task. Uncovering potential problems at the beginning provides the project team sufficient time to address these issues before they become critical, therefore eliminating costly surprises.

The same approach is needed in the sales process. An example of a costly sales surprise might be having your proposal thrown out at the last minute because of a concern raised by an influence you did not even know existed. Ever experience this heartbreak?

THREE ELEMENTS OF SYSTEMS

Effective systems are made up of three important elements. These are *innovation, quantification,* and *orchestration. Innovation* is the idea aspect of the process and possibly the most important element. Another way to think of innovation is as a proactive response to change. Until you try something, there is little need for the other two elements. *Quantification* is the scorekeeping process. This aspect is essential because, without it, you won't know what's happening.

"We need a plan here. From now on, Wimbish, you take the green states, Barkley, the yellow..."

The final element is *orchestration*, which is the systematic implementation of the best ideas into a duplicable process.

Let's review each of these elements and explore how they impact the selling process.

Innovation

Innovation should be applied to every aspect of the sales process. If you don't try different

> Method goes far to prevent trouble in business; for it makes the task easy, hinders confusion, saves abundance of time, and instructs those who have business depending, what to do and what to hope.
>
> —William Penn

techniques and strategies, you can't measure the different effects. Dr. Terry Paulson, the author of *They Shoot Managers, Don't They?*, said, "There is no off ramp to change." Since we can't avoid change, it is better to address it head on, and in the process retain some control.

Obstacles provide outstanding opportunities for innovation. The best salespeople look for obstacles. Why? Because the top salespeople realize an obstacle offers an opportunity to distinguish themselves from the competition. Innovation is testing different approaches to overcoming problems. Too often salespeople resist innovation. You hear comments like, "We've always done it this way before and it has always worked before, so why do I need to change?" With a changing world, unless we are constantly adapting, we are actually falling backwards.

Getting to the top. In prospecting, one challenge most salespeople can relate to is the problem of getting past a gatekeeper. Anthony Parinello developed an innovative approach to overcoming this obstacle. In his book, *Selling to VITO™, the Very Important Top Officer*, he describes a process of getting to VITO.

In a very abbreviated version, his plan calls for sending VITO a short letter. The letter is written on plain paper. That's right, he doesn't use stationery because he wants to avoid the prospect's prejudging. Right above VITO's name, there is large headline that offers a solution to a major challenge facing VITO. In closing, the letter says the salesperson will call VITO's assistant—named personally—at a

Creative Attention Getter

Here's a technique to get through to the hard-to-reach prospect that I'm sure the late actor Peter Sellers would admire.

In his book, *Fifty Ways to Close a Sale*, Gerald Michaelson says that he had a messenger deliver a 66" stuffed pink panther to the prospect's office. Attached was a tag reading, "You'll be tickled pink with the opportunity I have for you." When he called a few days later and identified himself, Michaelson got right through. Since then, he's sent out dozens of stuffed animals and other novelties to get prospects' attention.

specific time with more information and, if VITO is interested, he or she should take the call.

Does it always work? No. But Parinello reports amazing success with his innovative approach to getting VITO's attention. Does this technique guarantee Parinello more sales? No, but it does improve his access to decision makers, which substantially improves the possibilities and chances of a favorable outcome. However, the key to Parinello's sales success is that he continues to use innovation throughout the entire sales process.

The ultimate in Peppers and Rogers one-to-one marketing approach aligns you and your customer's visions of the future. While several companies may face the same problems and require the same solutions, few will share the same vision. By aligning with a top executive's vision for the future, you will create a unique relationship. This opens all kinds of opportunities to create value that never existed before. But without innovation, this isn't possible.

Quantification

Quantification is scorekeeping. Without measurement, no one would know what is going on. Some salespeople resist the idea of hard data, because they are afraid that their sales managers will use it against them. The problem is, they are often deceiving themselves and wondering why their sales results and commissions aren't better.

Can you imagine watching a basketball game without baskets on the backboards? Instead, the teams shoot at the backboard, and at the end of the game, the referee declares the winner to be the team that she "thought" played better. I doubt if people would find this version of the game as exciting or interesting as the current version. Yet, many salespeople prefer to take their sales shots without keeping score.

Hard information is essential because people's

> When you create an alliance with the vision, values, and core competencies of your customers, their business becomes your business. Their dreams become your dreams. Their goals become your opportunities. By understanding who they are and where they are going, you can say, 'This is how I can help you get there.'
>
> —Barbara Geraghty, *Visionary Selling*

perceptions don't always reflect reality. For example, a consultant asked retail employees with whom he was working: "What percentage of the people who come into your store make a purchase?" The employees estimated 80%. When the consultant forced them to keep actual records, they learned the actual figure was only about 20%!

This example introduces an important aspect of the quantification process. It is absolutely essential that you measure the results you are currently obtaining. Without this baseline, it is impossible to know if your innovations are an improvement or not. In the above situation, if the consultant had not forced the retailer to measure his initial results, a recommendation that would have increased the conversion factor to 50% might have been rejected because of the incorrectly perceived 80% conversion factor.

Benefits for planning. Another practical advantage of quantification is that it allows you to plan. For example, a real estate broker runs an advertisement in the Sunday paper on a split-level house, in a certain price range, in a certain neighborhood and expects to get 45 to 55 phone calls on Monday morning. She knows this because every time she runs a similar ad she gets that response. She also knows that one person can only handle between five and six phone calls per hour. Therefore, she knows she needs several salespeople knowledgeable about the advertised property to answer the phone Monday morning.

TESTING: 1, 2, 3

The wisdom of experimenting and measuring results was shown in a multimedia experiment by The Dallas Marketing Group.

To obtain qualified leads for the Fritztile Industries' commercial tile division, ads were placed in three trade magazines. One of three different letters was then mailed to each subscriber. One letter included a copy of the ads, another included a promotional product, and the third included a promotional product incentive offer. Which worked best? The letter with a promotional product incentive offer received an impressive 9.55% response.

—PS Ad Research

Yet how often have sales and marketing efforts been uncoordinated? One person ends up trying to answer all the calls. Most prospects can't get through because the line is always busy. Those who get through are confronted by people who know nothing about the property. Both results are disastrous for those trying to build relationships with their prospects.

Another important aspect of quantification is that it allows you to track the demographics and psychographics of your customers. Vilfredo Pareto observed the 80/20 rule. In this context, it means that 20% of your customers generate 80% of your profits, which means that not all customers are equal. Therefore, by concentrating on the top 20% of your customers or prospects who fit the profile of your best customers, you substantially improve the effectiveness of your sales efforts.

Demographics and Psychographics Defined

The difference between demographics and psychographics can be defined as what's outside a person's head versus what's inside a person's head.

Demographics are the differences between people (or companies) based on observable characteristics (age, race, income, and so forth).

Psychographics are differences between people (or companies) based on psychological factors. For instance, people can be grouped as seekers of price versus seekers of quality.

Orchestration

The last element is orchestration. This is where the salesperson develops an implementation plan to systematize the activities essential for a successful sale. Unfortunately, too often salespeople resist orchestration, because they believe it will cramp their style, remove their flexibility, destroy their spontaneity, and turn them into robots. Actually, it is just the opposite. Instead, think of orchestration as an ordered checklist for success.

Look at it this way. Astronauts are among the mostly highly trained and educated professionals

Following a Plan Works

MSA Consulting and Computer Services was nearly bankrupt. Two sales strategies helped turn it around.

One strategy was "Sell in the Treetops": Salespeople work hard to get their foot in the door near the top of the corporate hierarchy. They figure it makes it harder for someone further down the line to overturn a sale.

If they can't get in near the top, they look for an "angel," an internal advocate in the prospect company who wants to help them sell their services.

This new plan turned the company around—it was sold for $333 million and created many spin-offs and millionaires.

—Rick Crandall, *1001 Ways to Market Your Services: Even If You Hate to Sell*

in the world. And despite the fact they could probably perform their preflight activities in their sleep, they use a very detailed checklist to insure that nothing is omitted or performed out of order. If these top pilots rely on a checklist, should you as a top sales professional do anything less?

In their book *The New Strategic Selling*, Stephen Heiman and Diane Sanchez equate having a selling system to strategic planning. They have discovered that too often salespeople only concentrate on the tactical portion of the selling process, which they define as activities performed in direct contact with the prospect. They readily admit tactical skills are essential to the selling process, but they argue that the addition of strategic planning can substantially improve the probability of a sale in today's complex sales environment.

This is exactly the same as the basketball coach developing a game plan. The coach realizes that players must effectively execute the fundamentals (the tactical skills)—passing, rebounding, dribbling, and shooting—or they will have little chance of winning. But, in order to improve their chances of winning, the coach develops a game plan. The plan consists of ways his team can exploit its strengths and the other team's weaknesses. At the same time the coach attempts to minimize the impact of his team's weaknesses and the strengths of the other team. Often the weaker team in the fundamental skills wins because they have, and execute, a better game plan.

Buying influences. In *The New Strategic Sell-*

ing, Heiman and Sanchez develop a process with red flags that act as warnings of possible problems to the sale. Their process uses a checklist of what they call Buying Influences and Buyer Responses. They emphasize this checklist is necessary to avoid overlooking situations that could cause the loss of a sale.

The first Buying Influence is the Economic Buyer, who is the person responsible for final approval. There is always one and only one Economic Buyer per sale. The second Buying Influence is the User Buyer. These are the people who will use or be directly impacted by the product or service. There can be more than one User Buying Influence per sale.

> **Buying Influences**
> Have I involved the:
> ☑ economic buyer
> ☑ user buyer
> ☐ technical buyer
> ☐ coaching influences
>
> **Buyer Responses**
> What do they need:
> ☑ testimonials
> ☐ reliability data
> ☐ maintenance schedules

The third influence is the Technical Buyer and, again, there can be more than one of these per sale. These people can include accountants, attorneys, engineers, and others. They usually can't say yes, but can say no. Unfortunately, they too often exercise that right. The final Buying Influence is what they call Coaching Influences. These are people who are focusing on the salesperson's success with the particular sale. The coaches usually provide the salesperson with valuable information about the prospective company and its Buying Influences.

Buyer response modes. In addition to the multiple Buying Influences, Heiman and Sanchez identify four response modes: growth, trouble, even keel, and overconfident. Because different individuals use different response modes in identical situations, Heiman and Sanchez recommend a system to track each person. Unfortunately, too often salespeople assume all buyers are alike, which often causes a sale to be lost. In fact they say, "You need a 'safety line' to keep you properly oriented as you navigate through the maze of your sales opportunities."

Keep in mind that a system provides a floor, not a ceiling, for your activities. The purpose of the system is to insure certain minimal predictable results. The goal of a system is to standardize the routine tasks, which frees you to concentrate on the unique differences in every sales relationship. Another major advantage of using a system is that when something goes wrong and you don't get the desired result, it is much easier to zero in on the problem. Too often when a system is not in place, no one is aware of differences. The salespeople merely know they didn't get the sale. The problem is they don't know what to adjust in the next sales presentation.

IMPLEMENTING INNOVATION IN YOUR SALES SYSTEM

Often people think they are not capable of being innovative, but it is really a simple four-step process. The steps include the following:

(1) **Identify** the area you want to improve or the obstacle you want to overcome.

(2) **Measure** how you are doing at present.

(3) **Evaluate** the current condition to determine how you can minimize the variance.

(4) **Take action** to improve by implementing your best ideas.

Creative Ideas Rise Above Commodities

Jack Ryel, a purchasing manager for Phillips 66 Company, finds his suppliers similar on quality and price. He looks for those who bring creative solutions with them. For instance, one salesperson came up with a new money-saving freight program that grouped loads through a third-party vendor.

—*Sales & Marketing Executive Report*

Identifying the Problem

Logically, identifying the problem is the first step, but it is surprising how often this step is omitted. If you are even considering skipping this step, let me remind you how difficult it is to get the right answer when you are working on the wrong problem.

Obstacles can take many forms. Difficult gatekeepers have already been mentioned. Another problem is getting inaccurate feedback from your contacts at the prospect's company. For example, you may be told your product costs too much, while the real problem is that a technical advisor has concerns about some aspect of your product's performance. These two examples represent challenges that most salespeople are familiar with and address on a daily basis.

Problems make sales. The obstacles that present the most valuable challenge to you are the prospect's problems. These are the issues addressed by Parinello and Geraghty. The advantage is that when you handle these challenges effectively, you separate yourself from the majority of salespeople. These customer problems range from shrinking sales, to deteriorating quality control, to rising production costs—depending on your customers.

Measure Where You Start

Once you have identified the problem, you must concentrate on establishing a baseline from which to measure your future innovations. This is done by measuring your current performance

Defining Problems Is Key to Solving Them

When Einstein was asked how he would approach the problem of avoiding the end of the world if he had one hour to solve it, he said he'd spend 55 minutes identifying the problem and the last 5 minutes solving it. As Einstein said, ". . . the formulation of a problem is often far more essential than its solution."

Roger Firestien, of the Center for the Study of Creativity at Buffalo State College, says to try to phrase the problem using phrases like, "How could we . . . ," or "In what ways could we . . ."

Problem statements block creative thinking. Questions describe a problem that can be solved.

or the data obtained about your prospect's current performance.

Evaluate Current Conditions

The third step is evaluation. This is probably the most difficult step because you must determine what results you can reasonably obtain and compare them to your current results. With this knowledge, you must develop a method to close the gap. In the case of the prospect's problem, you must determine how your product or service can best improve their performance.

Take Action

Don't get hung up trying to find the ultimate solution. You will never know what that is until you try various approaches. Innovation is about constant change; therefore, it is better to improve a little at a time. If you try to implement big changes, you might do more harm than good. With little improvements constantly, you can adjust until you zero in on the best solution. For example, if you make a 1% improvement each week, you will have over a 50% improvement by the end of the year with a minimum negative impact from ideas that didn't work.

Ongoing experimentation. Your prospects and clients are sources of ideas to improve your service. Ask your prospects, "What can I do to make the buying process easier?" Or ask your current customers, "What made the difference in your selecting our product or service?" The answer to these questions will give you a better idea of your strengths, which you can then stress in your future sales presentations. Also, you will learn what weaknesses you have to work on. For example, you might have a contract that is basically very fair but very difficult to understand, so prospects may be afraid to commit.

Taking action is the "last" innovation and the most important. Without this step, all the rest have been a waste of time. Don't be afraid your innovations won't work. Each attempt gives you new information which lets you start the experimentation process again from a stronger foundation. Some will work and others won't, but what's important is to keep trying. You will always be improving.

SUMMARY

A sales system is not a silver bullet. Success in sales, even with a sales system, requires hard work and many sales skills. However, a sales system offers you immediate benefits in two areas.

First, a system allows you to identify and concentrate on your best prospects to insure the best use of your time and effort. Second, it allows you to organize the selling process for maximum effectiveness. This is critical today as the selling process has become increasingly complex. By organizing the sales process, you are able to counter threats to sales by working from a position of strength.

A sales system is not a straitjacket. It is a tool that allows you to be more innovative. It is a score

On Measurement

What is the major problem? It is fundamentally the confusion between effectiveness and efficiency that stands between doing the right things and doing things right. There is surely nothing quite so useless as doing with great efficiency what should not be done at all. Yet our tools—especially our accounting concepts and data—all focus on efficiency. What we need is (1) a way to identify the areas of effectiveness (of possible significant results), and (2) a method for concentrating on them . . . .

This is true of the marketplace. A handful of customers out of many thousands produce the bulk of the orders; a handful of products out of hundreds of items in the line produce the bulk of the volume; and so on. This is true of markets, end uses, and distributive channels. It is equally true of sales efforts: a few salesmen, out of several hundred, always produce two-thirds or more of all new business.

—Peter F. Drucker,
Peter Drucker on the Profession of Management

card that allows you to keep track of the many initiatives and actions necessary to make a sale. With a score card, you can track the status of your many initiatives, which will include ideas from earlier chapters in this book as well as some of your favorite sale techniques—ones you have already mastered.

Many sports metaphors are used in selling. However, unlike in sports, the successful sale must produce two winners: the seller *and* buyer. You are not in competition with your prospect. Instead you must work with your prospects to create the best solution for both of you. This lets you build a long-term business of referrals and repeat business. Without these, in the end *you* will lose.

In the long run, maybe the biggest benefit of a sales system is the sense of control it gives you. This is important because psychological studies have indicated that our sense of well being is directly proportional to our sense of control over our environment. By implementing a sales system, you can begin to make sales more fun.

> True control comes from a very few simple measures of high integrity understood by everybody and focused on the right stuff.
>
> —Tom Peters

BURST INTO ACTION

"Take time to deliberate, but when the time for action has arrived, stop thinking and go in."

—Napoleon Bonaparte

(1) Decide how to start implementing a systematic approach to your selling.

(2) List the variables you can creatively experiment with such as what you say to prospects, how you keep in touch with current customers, etc.

(3) List the demographics and psychographics of your ideal customers.

(4) What groups are your customers members of? Which of your customers would be happy to introduce you to more people like them?

(5) Decide what you will start measuring to see if you are on track. Sources of new prospects? Sources of referrals? How many contacts until a decision?

(6) Create a checklist of the process you go through to build relationships with prospects. Do the same for relationships with customers. Perhaps a flow chart for the wall would work better for you.

(7) Who else in your office needs to be considered in your sales process? The boss, others who answer the phone, your assistant?

(8) How can you improve your one-to-one relationship building with prospects and customers? Develop three specific tools to build your relationships. They can be from other chapters such as a needs analysis form, sending a newsletter or clippings, or a campaign of visiting networking groups.

INDEX